"The individual and collective quest we all pursue as educators to lift student achievement is complicated by a blizzard of theories and no lack of self-appointed experts. It is so exciting to see the years of serious, credible, and successful work that Jay Westover and his team have done with countless school districts captured in a way that is accessible to all of us committed to student success. It is an important book that reveals meaningful, capacity building paths for district and school leaders."

Jack O'Connell, former California State
Superintendent of Public Instruction

"*Districts on the Move* provides educators with critical insights into capacity building, which remains the holy grail for school districts in order to sustain the collaborative culture of inquiry that results in an organization focused on continuous improvement."

David Cash, former School District Superintendent and
EDL Program Governance Chair, USC Rossier School of Education

"*Districts on the Move* is a book about how school districts build systems of improvement that are larger than a person or an idea. The challenge for superintendents and district leaders is creating a culture and system of improvement that survives changes in leadership. Jay Westover's book provides both a framework and case study examples of how district leaders can create systemic improvements that show up on the desks of students in classrooms."

Cary Matsuoka, Santa Barbara USD Superintendent

"This body of work is a must-read for every educational leader, especially at the central office level. There are no easy answers to address equity in education, but there are intentional ways to build coherence and lead the work. Jay Westover has created a clear and precise framework for building capacity for whole systems change that starts from the desk of the student and moves throughout the organization. This is not a read one time kind of book, but rather a guiding resource for leaders to use in order to successfully meet the needs of all students."

Karen Valdes, former member of the California
State Board of Education

"Improvement efforts in education have prompted reforms intended to ensure that teachers and school leaders have the professional skill set and capacity to meet the educational needs of all students. However, where others have failed, InnovateEd has succeeded, creating explicit structures for school and district collaboration that develop a shared learning system of interaction. *Districts on the Move* enables both increased technical expertise and organic accountability systems in which dialectic practices about student learning result in strengthening of collective agreements. Professional learning in this kind of setting is purposeful and directly connected to student learning outcomes."

Patricio Vargas, Norwalk La Mirada Unified School District
Assistant Superintendent, Educational Services

"As a teacher, principal, or district office administrator, *Districts on the Move* will give you a new way to look at your work. Jay Westover knows people make the difference in organizations. Systemic collaboration and co-learning leads to continuous improvement for students. Every educator has realized we can no longer be successful alone. *Districts on the Move* details a step-by-step process of collective implementation with practical examples every educator can use."

Joni Howard, Corona-Norco Unified School District
Elementary School Principal

"Jay Westover and the InnovateEd team have been working and learning with school districts for a number of years. He understands deeply that schools want their students to do better, and that school districts can make a great difference in inspiring, leading, and learning with schools to become more precise about the work on the students' desks. This book illuminates powerful, practical pathways for districts and schools to increase their impact and accelerate and deepen learning for students and staff. It is a must-read for all educators who want to become better at what really matters in our classrooms."

Mary Jean Gallagher, Chief Student Achievement Officer and
Assistant Deputy Minister (retired), Ministry of Education
for Ontario, Canada

Districts on the Move

To my parents, Jerry and Lois Westover, who dedicated their working years as classroom teachers to better the lives of students in their care. Family, friends, and former students have cherished their support, guidance, and companionship. It is my hope to leave a legacy that positively impacts as many people as they have over the past 86 years and counting.

To my wife, Erin, and children, Mackenzie, Katie, and Jacob, whose love and support I am forever grateful for as they are my daily inspiration for improving school districts so that all students are well prepared for college, career, and life.

Districts on the Move

Leading a Coherent System
of Continuous Improvement

Jay Westover

Foreword by Michael Fullan and Joanne Quinn

A JOINT PUBLICATION

A SAGE Publishing Company

FOR INFORMATION:

Corwin

A SAGE Company

2455 Teller Road

Thousand Oaks, California 91320

(800) 233-9936

www.corwin.com

SAGE Publications Ltd.

1 Oliver's Yard

55 City Road

London, EC1Y 1SP

United Kingdom

SAGE Publications India Pvt. Ltd.

B 1/I 1 Mohan Cooperative Industrial Area

Mathura Road, New Delhi 110 044

India

SAGE Publications Asia-Pacific Pte. Ltd.

18 Cross Street #10-10/11/12

China Square Central

Singapore 048423

Publisher: Arnis Burvikovs

Development Editor: Desirée A. Bartlett

Senior Editorial Assistant: Eliza Erickson

Production Editor: Tori Mirsadjadi

Copy Editor: Sarah J. Duffy

Typesetter: Hurix Digital

Proofreader: Susan Schon

Indexer: Jeanne R. Busemeyer

Cover Designer: DallyVerghese

Marketing Manager: Sharon Pendergast

ISBN 978-1-5443-8762-8

This book is printed on acid-free paper.

19 20 21 22 23 10 9 8 7 6 5 4 3 2 1

Contents

Foreword

By Michael Fullan and Joanne Quinn
Authors and Consultants

Our book *Coherence: The Right Drivers in Action for Schools, Districts, and Systems* (Fullan & Quinn, 2016) hit a responsive chord. Fullan had written a policy paper in 2011 titled "Choosing the Wrong Drivers for Whole System Reform," in which he cited punitive accountability, individualism, technology, and fragmented initiatives as policies that not only failed to improve things, but actually made them worse. Fullan briefly offered some ideas for the "right drivers." The reaction to the paper was one of excitement, but readers clearly wanted more guidance.

Since 2011, we have conducted a large number of workshops with schools and districts where we fleshed out the right drivers—hence the book, *Coherence*. In our work supporting systems, we try to offer the most complete solution without becoming so complex that it becomes overwhelming to use in practice. We call this "simplexity," which is not a real word but is a good concept. It means that you take a complex problem and boil it down to the smallest number of essential concepts that explain the phenomenon. The simple part is that there are few elements and they can be explained. The complex part is how to synergize them in action. Thus, we offered a Coherence Framework as illustrated in Figure 1 (Fullan & Quinn, 2016).

We suggested that successful systems combine and interrelate four components: focusing direction, cultivating collaborative cultures, deepening learning, and securing accountability. The role of leadership at all levels is to synergize the four elements. We stressed that it is not a step-by-step model. For example, you cannot effectively focus direction without engaging in collaboration. We found that the best metaphor is the pulsating heart—there are four chambers; if blood is not flowing within and across all four chambers, the system will not work or will break down.

In any case, *Coherence* became an instant best seller and is still going strong. We have had numerous responses to the effect that the book really captures the solution, and countless study groups have formed. At first blush readers say, "Finally we have an answer to overload and initiativitis." But then a new reality sets in. *Coherence* is the new how, but when people work with it they quickly realize that the new problem is how to do the how. In the book we hinted at the actual solution when we defined coherence as "the shared depth of understanding about the purpose and nature of the work" (Fullan & Quinn, 2016, p. 16). Right away you know that you can't get individual depth, let alone shared depth, by reading and discussing a book, by listening to an inspiring speech, or by attending a good workshop. Shared depth is what happens or does not happen between workshops. It has to do with changing the culture toward daily, purposeful, specific interaction. It requires careful development of precision of pedagogy. It depends on collaborative cultures that have certain characteristics (many schools have weak or nonexistent collaboration), and if you try to insist on or prescribe the nature of collaboration you land right back in "wrong driver" land.

So the big question that remains is: How do we comprehensively implement the good ideas in the coherence framework? We got a hint when we compared alignment to coherence. Alignment is when you identify the key pieces: vision, goals, strategy, curriculum, budget, professional development, assessment, and so on. When comparing this with what we had in mind (e.g., shared depth of understanding), it immediately occurred to us that alignment is rational while coherence is emotional. Emotions stick; rational ideas don't. What would be necessary for ideas to stick would be experiencing the ideas with others sorting out what works and what doesn't.

We also later realized that achieving coherence is not a state. Instead, it is a process of continuous coherence-making. Even if you do a lot of coherence-making at the front end, your job is not finished for at least three reasons. First, people come and go all the time. Every newcomer is a coherence-making proposition. Second, state policies and/or environments change. Third, hopefully the group has new ideas along the way. All of these require new coherence-making capacities.

Most of all, we found out that people and groups needed assistance, especially at the beginning. They need help in developing leadership and assessing how well they are doing. This help must be ongoing in the early stages. Our team was doing some of this, but it was clear that we were limited in our capacity to work with even a fraction of those who wanted more help. It was at that time that we started to work with Jay Westover and InnovateEd. They saw the value of the Coherence Framework and also recognized that hardly anyone was working on school district capacity building as distinct from individual school turnaround. For the past four years, we have been working with InnovateEd to help them develop their capacity to support district coherence-making on an increasingly large scale. They have developed a framework for systemic improvement called *Districts on the Move,* going well beyond what we are able to do in both ideas and capacity (Westover, 2018).

The book you are about to read is the first full version of these new applied ideas. You will see that InnovateEd has developed what they call "creating a coherent system of continuous improvement." They have established the Benchmarks of Capacity framework for school district coherence. They have zeroed in on leadership for coherence in a deeper and more comprehensive way than we were able to do. Most importantly, they have been co-learning with many districts to identify coherent pathways of progress. In so doing, they have developed four Benchmarks of Capacity and 12 Leadership Competencies. They also show that what really counts is having a culture of shared leadership.

Jay and his team have taken our advice and dug deeper to establish greater precision while avoiding either extreme of leaving things too vague or being too prescriptive. They have done this for both key aspects of any effective change model: pedagogy and change leadership (or, if you prefer, improvement strategies). They also help people get better incrementally by showing how short cycles of improvement lead to increasingly greater impact.

All of this groundwork is done clearly and succinctly, but what makes it more convincing is the series of four named district case studies—the very districts that were the test-beds of co-development and co-discovery. All of this enables Jay to pull together what has been learned and how it paves the way for further developments, including a coherent instructional framework, a continuous improvement cycle, use of evidence to inform impact, establishing sustainable growth, and a complete set of rubrics and tools to guide further work.

In short, it has become quite clear that coherence-making will be needed even more so in the future, that districts need external assistance to move forward, that such assistance must be aimed at building internal capacity to lead coherence-making, and finally, and crucially, it is systems (districts not individual schools) that must develop their capacity. InnovateEd's systems work is comprehensive and builds internal capacity to enhance greater self-determination while at the same time cultivating districts to network with other districts. The desire and capacity of districts to learn individually and with other systems becomes the most powerful outcome.

Figure 1   The Coherence Framework

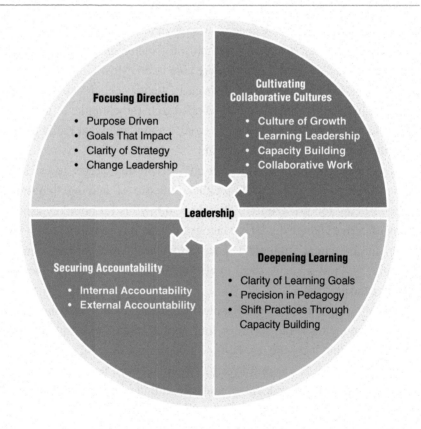

Preface

The education landscape in the United States has changed under the auspices of the Every Student Succeeds Act. This new vision for education has afforded the opportunity for school district leaders, principals, and teachers to have local control for achieving the equitable improvement of student learning outcomes. However, this transition has a dichotomous challenge in that leading systemic improvement requires a clearly delineated, multiyear strategy for creating a coherent system of continuous improvement. Leaders at every level of the school district will need to collectively engage in improvement efforts with a common focus on developing cultures, building capacity, and creating coherent systems.

After having been an education practitioner for 25 years, and leading systemic district improvement for the past 15 years, I have seen educational research and evidence-based practices evolve to set the stage for deeper and more systemic district improvement. And so it was simpatico that in 2015 the work of Michael Fullan and Joanne Quinn came to serve as a compatible framework for further improving the ongoing efforts of creating coherent systems of continuous improvement, later published as *Coherence* (Fullan & Quinn, 2016), which has resonated with educators at large. A synergistic collaboration with InnovateEd and Fullan and Quinn began four years ago and continues to expand with positive results for district leaders, principals, teachers, and students in their care.

This book was written in response to the key learnings that have been refined over the past 15 years of partnering with school districts focused on the sustainable improvement of leadership, teaching, and student learning. Educators who will most benefit from this book are those who recognize and embrace school district improvement as a long-term journey that requires integration of efforts at the district, school, and classroom levels to realize the equitable improvement of student learning outcomes. And those who have read *Coherence* will have the right mindset for focusing direction, cultivating a collaborative culture, deepening student learning, and securing internal accountability. Two key questions are intended as critical takeaways from this book to guide educators at every level with leading a collective vision of long-term success:

1. How does a school district navigate a path of progress for the sustainable improvement of culture, capacity, and coherence?

2. Which critical success factors guide the leadership at all levels of a school district to maximize the impact of teaching on student learning?

There has been a keen eye with special attention for staying true to the guiding principle that school district improvement efforts must focus on three essential elements: developing cultures, building capacity, and creating coherence. There is no recipe or step-by-step solution for leading systemic improvement; rather, long-term success is dependent on developing leadership capacity at all levels to guide the continuous improvement of practices and student learning results. Every school district has a distinct starting point from which to forge a unique path of progress influenced by a legacy culture, internal capacity, and the degree of systemic coherence. In an effort to navigate the complexities of school district improvement, this book includes case studies of how districts progressed over time, leadership competencies shown to be critical factors for success, tools and rubrics for action planning and guiding implementation, and reflective questions for inquiring about the current state of district systems and practices as well as clearly delineating strategies for systemic improvements efforts.

The book chapters are designed as a roadmap with guideposts that serve as a framework for school districts to create a coherent system of continuous improvement. Chapter 1 sets the stage by introducing the Benchmarks of Capacity for school district coherence and Leadership Competencies for creating coherence that are further delineated in subsequent chapters. Chapter 2 provides guidance and actionable tools for leading the equitable growth of student learning through clearly delineated strategies driven by recurring cycles of improvement. Chapter 3 focuses on how to develop shared leadership and systemic collaboration at the district, school, and classroom levels by serving as lead learners that promote a culture of leading from the middle. Chapter 4 provides guidance and actionable tools for creating instructional coherence through robust collaborative inquiry processes that develop precision of pedagogy and improved student learning results. Chapter 5 clarifies how to lead the continuous improvement of practices at the district, school, and classroom levels through evidence-based inquiry cycles informed by lag outcomes, lead metrics, and student success indicators. Chapter 6 provides guidance for both action planning and monitoring implementation with rubrics and tools designed to navigate a coherent path focused on the continuous improvement of systems, practices, and student learning outcomes.

Education practitioners may find this book to be a valuable resource for professional learning, leadership development, or shaping of systemic improvement strategies at the district and school levels. However, there is a more important reason to read this book. For too long in the field of education there has been a fragmented approach to school district improvement emanating from disconnected efforts between the central office and school sites as well as competing interests among schools within the district. The intent of this book is to guide school districts in a more systemic process that creates a coherent system of continuous improvement by developing leadership capacity at all levels. Our hope is that district leaders, principals, and teachers utilize this book as a common reference for leading a collective path of progress as a *District on the Move*.

Acknowledgments

nnovateEd was founded in 2007 by Lynn Hodson and Jay Westover to fulfill the vision of serving as strategic school district partners for the challenging endeavor of building capacity to create coherent systems of continuous improvement. The amazing and talented team at InnovateEd has grown over time, and their collective expertise and dedication to the work of school districts is cherished and valued. We cannot thank them enough: Don Ward, Nancy Hubbell, Vanessa de Guzman, Marianna Vinson, Wendy Davoud, Kira Shearer, Jennie Wright, Sharon McCreight, Nancy Padilla, Debra Kaplan, Marcie Poole, Amy Bryant, Mary Buttler, Sharon Wright, Monica Trousdale, Kara Duros, RoseMarie Hickman, Jill Bradford, Jean Castruita, Kristen Buczek, Ken Greenhaum, Cheryl Krehbiel, Jenn Padilla, Tiffany Walker, Angela Macias, and Heidi Boley.

Michael Fullan, Joanne Quinn, and Mary Jean Gallagher have been invaluable collaborators and partners over the past four years for both the InnovateEd team and school districts that have engaged in the journey of becoming a *District on the Move*. We have learned much from their collective knowledge, firsthand experience, and leading-edge research on whole-systems change.

Most of all, we greatly appreciate the leadership of our long-term district partners who demonstrate a steadfast and moral imperative for the equitable improvement of student learning outcomes. It is the daily work of district leaders, principals, and teachers that collectively creates a coherent system of continuous improvement as *Districts on the Move*.

PUBLISHER'S ACKNOWLEDGMENTS

Corwin gratefully acknowledges the contributions of the following reviewers

Lisa Simon
Associate Superintendent, Educational Services
Norco, CA

David Cash
Professor, Retired Superintendent
Long Beach, CA

Karen L. Tichy
Assistant Professor of Educational Leadership
St Louis, MO

Jill Gildea
Superintendent
Park City, UT

About the Author

Jay Westover has provided leadership training and school improvement consulting in collaboration with the U.S. Department of Education, state departments of education, colleges, educational service centers, and school districts across North America. Over the past 15 years, his work has focused on developing capacity of school district systems to close the gaps of college and career readiness. Creating coherent systems of continuous improvement has been a central aspect of statewide, regional, and local partnerships including the Association of California School Administrators, more than a dozen county offices of education, and over 100 school districts.

Jay's role at InnovateEd is lead advisor for state, county, and local school district partnerships; client executive leadership coaching; and guiding the expansion of consulting services. His passion is working alongside leaders to simplify the complexities of developing school district capacity and coherence for sustainable improvement.

Introduction

· ·

Having partnered with school districts over the past 15 years in support of capacity-building efforts, I have seen the emergence of a simple yet powerful concept for the sustainable improvement of student learning. The long-term success of school districts requires a systemic approach for creating a coherent system of continuous improvement (Westover, 2018). The reason is that the district is the most important unit of system change, not the school by itself.

What is needed for success is a change in the *culture* of learning, and the district is the best context for this to happen on any scale. In the same way that if you change only one classroom you don't change the school, when you change one school you don't change the district. More than this, if one school gets changed in the absence of district change, it typically doesn't stay changed. When we say that the key is change in the culture of learning, we mean changes in the way students and teachers learn and changes in how relationships within the district develop to support learning for *all students*. The nature of such change includes three elements.

1

First, teachers begin to work effectively in teams to support each other in focused student learning led by principals and teacher leaders as lead learners. Second, district leaders develop coordinated teams at the district level, who in turn develop two-way relationships with schools focused on the core agenda of learning. Third, districts and schools together find ways for schools to learn from each other laterally. Overall it is this *systemness of purposeful and ongoing interaction* that produces gains in student learning.

However, a deep understanding of the progression in school district improvement is needed to navigate the complexities of changing district culture and practices. School districts demonstrating the clarity, commitment, collaboration, and accountability needed to create a coherent system of continuous improvement are deemed *Districts on the Move*. We use the phrase *on the move* because forward motion is essential for coherence-making and continuous improvement, as both necessitate constant adapting and adjusting to realize the equitable improvement of student learning outcomes.

The California Network of Districts on the Move was established in 2014 by InnovateEd in collaboration with the Association of California School Administrators as a statewide strategy for building capacity of school districts to lead whole-systems change. Beginning in 2015, Michael Fullan and Joanne Quinn came to serve as lead advisors of the network and continue to be instrumental in integrating the four drivers of the Coherence Framework for systems improvement. In 2016, the network was selected by the California Collaborative for Educational Excellence to become one of the first statewide learning networks to support school districts with leading the equitable improvement of student learning outcomes.

InnovateEd continues to lead the expansion of *Districts on the Move* driven by the mission of developing school district capacity and coherence for sustainable improvement of leadership, teaching, and student learning. Urban, suburban, and rural districts ranging from 2,000 to 100,000 students have joined the network and over time have built capacity and created coherence guided by the Benchmarks of Capacity and Leadership Competencies.

As of 2018, a total of 30 school districts comprising 700 schools serving approximately 600,000 students have engaged in the journey of becoming a *District on the Move* to realize the equitable improvement of student learning outcomes. The vision of InnovateEd is to have a long-term impact on education that is realized through the collective efforts of district leaders, principals, and teachers as they strive to create coherent systems of continuous improvement as *Districts on the Move*.

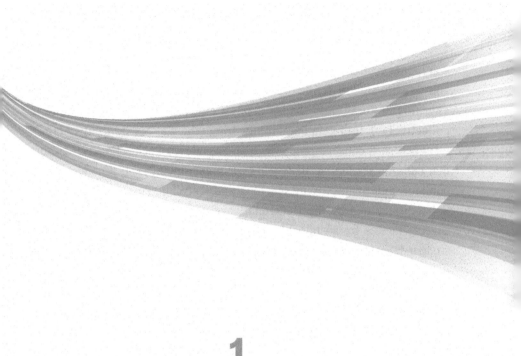

1

Creating a Coherent System of Continuous Improvement

· ·

E very school district has a unique culture and varied degrees of capacity at the district, school, and classroom levels to guide the continuous improvement of teaching and learning. The complexities of capacity building become more apparent as school districts progress from a compliance orientation with cultural norms expressed as "this is something else for us to do" and "this too shall pass." The transition to a culture of leading from the middle emerges by empowering and equipping those with closer proximity to student learning, which results in comments such as "my ideas can have an impact on our collective work" and "we are able to define the support we need to be successful." Gradually, this cultural shift shapes a more coherent system that results in collectively defining and communicating "the way we do things here."

Each shift causes ripple effects in the fabric of school district culture that calls on leaders at all levels to navigate changes in practice with a common aim of improving teaching and learning. This path of progress is best illustrated by the Benchmarks of Capacity, which define critical success factors for sustainable improvement of leadership, teaching, and student learning. So how do the Benchmarks of Capacity distinguish a district as being on the move?

Foremost, a strategic focus based on the root causes of student inequity and underperformance clearly delineates improvement strategies connecting student success indicators with high-yield instructional practices and assessments for learning that, in turn, guides school site actions and district supports. In addition, formal structures and processes for systemic collaboration and co-learning among and between teachers, principals, and district leaders promotes a culture of leading from the middle and serving as lead learners for successful navigation of the ongoing improvement process. Most importantly, a coherent instructional framework that integrates curricular resources, instructional strategies, and assessments for learning provides guidance for three- to four-week instructional cycles. The purpose of which is developing precision of pedagogy to engage all students in rigorous and complex tasks using high-yield instructional practices informed by timely assessments for learning that results in improved student achievement. And to maintain focus, the setting of annual growth targets measured by local assessments inform district and school progress through clearly defined cycles of evidence-based collaborative inquiry at the classroom, school, and district levels. These systemic feedback loops guide the continuous improvement of practices and student learning results.

InnovateEd's Benchmarks of Capacity (Figure 1.1) provide a framework for school districts to implement strategies that build capacity and expertise within and among schools. This is essential as the improvement of district culture and practices always precedes growth in student learning results.

Figure 1.1   **Benchmarks of Capacity for School District Coherence**

Clarity of District Goals and School Priorities for Student Learning

A strategic focus based on the root causes of student inequity and underperformance clearly delineates improvement strategies connecting student success indicators with high-yield instructional practices and assessments for learning that in turn guide school site actions and district supports.

Culture of Shared Leadership and Systemic Collaboration

Formal structures and processes for systemic collaboration and co-learning among and between teachers, principals, and district leaders promotes a culture of leading from the middle and serving as lead learners, which results in successful navigation of the ongoing change process.

Coherent Instructional Framework for Developing Collective Expertise

A coherent instructional framework integrating curricular resources, instructional strategies, and assessments for learning provides guidance for three- to four-week instructional cycles that engage all students in rigorous and complex tasks using high-yield instructional practices informed by timely assessments for learning that results in precision of pedagogy and improved student achievement.

Evidence-based Inquiry Cycles for Continuous Improvement

Setting annual growth targets measured by local assessments informs district and school progress through evidence-based cycles of collaborative inquiry at the classroom, school, and district levels, which create feedback loops for the continuous improvement of practices and student learning results.

The short-lived nature of many district improvement efforts is often a result of focusing on improved student learning outcomes without attention to the depth of implementation needed to develop collective expertise for improving teaching and learning. School districts are more apt to sustain improvement efforts by benchmarking the progress of capacity-building strategies and monitoring the impact on student learning as this affords a long-term vision for growth in student learning outcomes.

LEADING A COHERENT PATH OF PROGRESS

The collective efforts of leaders at all levels is needed to cultivate a collaborative culture that focuses direction and develops collaborative expertise for deepening student learning. The culture of leadership in a school district is the most critical factor for both advancing progress and sustaining improvement efforts. The Benchmarks of Capacity serve as a framework for *Districts on the Move* to navigate a coherent path focused on the continuous improvement of leadership, teaching, and student learning. In addition, twelve Leadership Competencies (Figure 1.2) are essential for the long-term process of developing capacity and creating coherence for equitable improvement of student learning outcomes.

The development of these Leadership Competencies was a direct result of seeking a solution for a persistent challenge occurring in every school district: developing leadership at every level to collaboratively engage in the systemic improvement of district culture, capacity, and coherence. The intent of the Leadership Competencies is to foster a common understanding of the essential leadership actions for building capacity at every level of the district. The key for long-term success is maintaining a focus on creating coherence in spite of the daily urgent demands in schools that constantly pull leaders away from the important work of improving teaching and learning. There is no starting or ending point to creating coherence; rather, it is an ongoing and integrated approach for leaders at all levels to focus efforts on developing collaborative expertise.

Figure 1.2 Leadership Competencies for Building Capacity to Create Coherence

Clarity of District Goals and School Priorities for Student Learning

- ❏ Creating a strategic focus for equitable student growth
- ❏ Clearly delineating improvement strategies
- ❏ Leading short cycles of improvement

Culture of Shared Leadership and Systemic Collaboration

- ❏ Serving as a lead learner
- ❏ Cultivating systemic collaboration and co-learning
- ❏ Leading from the middle

Coherent Instructional Framework for Developing Collective Expertise

- ❏ Creating instructional coherence
- ❏ Fostering robust collaborative inquiry processes
- ❏ Developing precision of pedagogy

Evidence-based Inquiry Cycles for Continuous Improvement

- ❏ Knowing thy impact on equitable student learning outcomes
- ❏ Focusing evidence of learning on problems of practice
- ❏ Continuously improving practices through disciplined inquiry

In the forthcoming chapters, the Benchmarks of Capacity will illustrate these Leadership Competencies in action through school district case studies and research from the field. Creating a strategic focus for equitable student growth requires leaders to clearly delineate strategies for short cycles of improvement. A culture of shared leadership and systemic collaboration is cultivated by lead learners who model co-learning and promote leadership from the middle. A coherent instructional framework for developing collective expertise calls on leaders to create instructional coherence through robust collaborative inquiry processes that develop precision of pedagogy. And leaders guide evidence-based inquiry cycles for continuous improvement of practices using evidence of learning to know thy impact on the equitable improvement of student learning outcomes.

There are divergences in each school district's journey toward creating a coherent system of continuous improvement that stems from the current state of district culture and capacity. However, the convergent path of progress for *Districts on the Move* is illuminated by the Benchmarks of Capacity and realized by the Leadership Competencies for creating a more coherent system. What follows are the Leadership Competencies of each benchmark illustrated by research and district case studies to assist school and district leaders with creating coherent systems of continuous improvement.

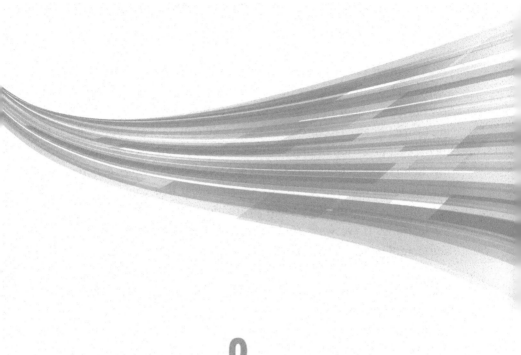

2

Clarity of District Goals and School Priorities for Student Learning

· ·

The challenge for educators is not the absence of district goals and school priorities for student learning. The issue at hand is a lack of clarity and precision that diminishes impact on the equitable improvement of student learning outcomes. There is a long-standing belief that district goals cascade onto school sites whose primary objective is aligning priorities to achieve annual student growth targets. This is a recipe for compliance-orientated school improvement, and we have decades of research to prove that this approach does not work. So why do we keep doing it?

The more promising approach occurs when school sites collectively define the desired impact of teaching and learning at the student desk to prioritize school improvement efforts that gradually result in achieving district goals. This creates a more coherent path of improvement that focuses on precision of practice and evidence of impact on student learning. School site actions and district supports become more coherent when leaders focus on short cycles of improvement that connect student success indicators with high-yield instructional practices and assessments for learning. If we want students to demonstrate success with rigorous and complex tasks, then instructional supports must focus on developing key cognitive strategies for applying content knowledge so that the impact on learning can be measured by authentic assessments of student learning priorities.

However, when driven only by district goals, the result is guiding statements such as "If we want students to demonstrate improved math performance, then we must provide multitiered systems of support so that impact on learning can be measured by quarterly benchmark assessments." When the focus is on the student desk, these statements become more precise: "If we want students to demonstrate the ability to create viable arguments and critique the reasoning of others, then instructional supports must gradually release students to engage in structured collaboration with evidence-based arguments so that impact on learning can be measured by the work produced by students." The equitable improvement of student learning will be realized only by improvement efforts that directly impact the student desk, and the first step for creating such a strategic focus is addressing the root causes of student inequity and underperformance: key cognitive strategies for applying content knowledge.

CREATING A STRATEGIC FOCUS FOR EQUITABLE STUDENT GROWTH

If a district is committed to the equitable improvement of student learning outcomes, then it is essential to examine the causal pathway that links annual goals for academic growth to lead metrics and student success indicators. In the same way that if your annual goal is to lose ten pounds, then the lead metric of progress is periodically weighing yourself. Success indicators are directly linked to caloric intake and routine exercise. The monitoring of weight gain or loss provides insight into the impact of caloric intake and exercise so that future actions can result in achieving the desired goal.

The diverse learning needs of students adds layers of complexity to the causal pathway linking short-term student progress with annual academic proficiency. A strategic focus for improving student learning is easier to attain when viewed through the lens of the key cognitive strategies for applying content knowledge shown in Figure 2.1.

Figure 2.1 Visible Evidence of Student Learning

Higher Order Thinking Skills

Students engage in rigorous and complex tasks requiring analysis, reasoning, evaluation, logic, problem solving, justifying, and transferring learning to new contexts via planning and creativity.

Close and Analytic Reading

Students access and interpret various media types with a clear purpose requiring annotation, source-dependent questions, note-taking, and analysis of information to gain knowledge for engaging in evidence-based conversations, writing, and performance tasks.

Precise Use of Academic Language

Students speak and write with precise use of general academic and domain-specific vocabulary, grammar, syntax, and word meaning as part of productive discourse related to content specific subject matter.

Structured Student Collaboration

Students effectively work in pairs or groups on clearly defined tasks with specific roles and responsibilities for engaging in structured academic discourse to convey understanding, share ideas, and build on the thoughts and reasoning of others.

Evidence-Based Arguments

Students develop claims, conjectures, and hypotheses that require analysis of information and interpretation of evidence to construct meaning, apply reasoning, and justify the logic of models.

Evidence-Based Writing

Students clearly communicate through short constructed responses and process writing across content areas for a variety of purposes and audiences to justify opinions and arguments with evidence, show understanding of concepts, and transfer learning to new contexts.

Focusing on what students can do with content knowledge allows evidence of student learning to become more visible. This is a shift from students showing what they know to students demonstrating what they can do. And this shift is the primary emphasis of current state standards that have elevated student learning to focus on more rigorous and complex student tasks.

Creating a strategic focus that guides school sites with improving student learning outcomes should involve a thorough examination of multiple data sets (or metrics) to determine root causes of variation in student learning. Instead there is a tendency to focus attention on annual lag outcomes rather than leading indicators of student progress. One common lag outcome is the annual assessment of student literacy such as the English Language Arts/Literacy Smarter Balanced Assessment. We equate this to weighing yourself at the end of the year.

Both of these measurements promote wide speculation and varied ideas as to what may have attributed to the measurable outcome. And without a laser sharp focus on the causal pathway of leading indicators, this results in vague solutions for a specific problem; "eat less and exercise more" is just as precise as "students need to read and write more and engage in research more frequently."

A more productive path is to engage in root cause analysis of visible evidence that denotes the leading indicators of improved student learning. For weight loss, the visible evidence is caloric intake and frequency or duration of exercise. Similarly, we would advocate that visible evidence of student learning is associated with the ability to demonstrate higher order thinking skills, close and analytic reading, precise use of academic language, structured collaboration, evidence-based arguments, and evidence-based writing. If we desire an equitable improvement in student literacy, then we must link this outcome with analyzing visible evidence of these leading indicators for student success.

This approach promotes in-depth collaborative inquiry to discern whether students' inability to use key cognitive strategies for applying content knowledge has had an impact on their progress toward academic proficiency. What are students not yet able to do with the content? To successfully complete rigorous and complex tasks, students must develop key cognitive skills for applying content knowledge as part of the ongoing learning process. The purpose, then, of analyzing evidence to discern the root causes of variance in student learning is to create a schoolwide focus that provides all students with support needed for developing key cognitive strategies as part of learning opportunities that occur in every classroom throughout the school year. The challenge of creating a strategic focus that improves learning for all students lies in the clarity and specificity needed for schoolwide implementation of agreed-upon improvement strategies.

CLEARLY DELINEATING IMPROVEMENT STRATEGIES

The process of defining a schoolwide instructional focus and identifying strategies for improving teaching and learning often yields a list of instructional strategies. Further, a strategic focus centered on teaching practices often results in improvement efforts that advocate for their consistent use in all classrooms. We call this *strategy rich and learning poor*. In time, such an approach can diminish the impact on student learning as school staff can fall trap to the cliché "I taught it, but students didn't learn it."

What is needed is a change in mindset of an improvement strategy to that of focusing job-embedded professional learning on a few student success indicators using high-yield instructional practices informed by timely assessments for learning. This shifts the dialogue to clarifying the common work and support needed for the continuous improvement of practices. The purpose, then, of an improvement strategy is engaging school staff in job-embedded professional learning that develops collective expertise to improve practices for attaining more equitable student learning outcomes.

A clearly delineated improvement strategy focuses the collective efforts of a school on the causal pathway for improving student learning. Five key questions provide guidance for schools to shape their improvement strategies:

1. Which student success indicators will result in the equitable improvement of student learning?

2. Which high-yield instructional practices will have the greatest impact on student learning?

3. How will assessments for learning inform the timely adjustment of instructional supports?

4. How can job-embedded professional learning be dedicated to developing collective expertise?

5. What time frames should guide our collective efforts through short improvement cycles focused on teaching and learning?

By sequentially responding to each question, a school is able to clearly delineate improvement strategies that create common ground for the collaborative work of teachers, site administrators, and district support staff. When linked together, these agreements form a coherent path for improving teaching and learning: developing collective expertise to improve student learning with high-yield instructional practices informed by timely assessments for learning.

The impact of an improvement strategy will be realized only if it results in taking action, as planning to improve can become an outcome in and of itself. Establishing time frames for short cycles of improvement promotes an action orientation for getting better together often referred to as *collaborative inquiry*. The role of school and district leaders must become one of co-leading short cycles of improvement guided by a clearly delineated implementation plan to develop collective expertise for deepening student learning.

LEADING SHORT CYCLES OF IMPROVEMENT

At the beginning of each school year, a sense of renewal and urgency is felt among educators as new students enter classrooms to engage in learning for continued academic growth. Student progress is celebrated and achievement gaps are realized. This sets the stage for establishing goals for annual student academic growth in spite of the uncertainty of not knowing the learning needs of each student. Unfortunately, when year-end goals are set in the absence of a clear path for improvement, the result is a lack of confidence among school staff for attaining student growth targets.

This recurring knowing–doing gap is a by-product of realizing that student academic growth is important, but not having the clarity needed to put into practice the instructional supports that will most impact student learning. This foundational challenge of improving practices to realize gains in student learning can be resolved only by actively participating in the process of learning what to do by co-leading improvement efforts (Pfeffer & Sutton, 2000). If school staff can approach student academic growth as short cycles of improvement, then high-yield instructional practices will emerge by engaging in three- to six-week cycles of collaborative inquiry for continuous improvement. The reality is that the path of progress for improved student academic growth does not have to be known at the beginning of the school year; rather, short cycles of improvement will define the path for teachers to maximize the impact on student learning.

If a school has a strategic focus for equitable improvement of student learning and has clearly delineated improvement strategies for developing collective expertise to deepen student learning, then the challenge for leaders is shaping school culture to engage in recurring cycles of improvement. This can be attained only by cultivating the capacity of teacher leaders to guide job-embedded professional learning of teacher teams within the school. The best approach for this capacity-building process is equipping and empowering school leadership teams to design an implementation plan that will guide their efforts of collaboratively leading short cycles of improvement; the author owns the plan.

The true impact of a school implementation plan is realized when at six-week intervals a school leadership team brings to the table key learnings from teacher teams so that the implementation plan can be refined with improved specificity of student learning needs and increased precision of instructional supports. For this to happen, the school principal will need to serve as a lead learner developing shared leadership and systemic collaboration within the school. Teachers will rise to the occasion when principals promote a culture of leading from the middle that empowers and equips school staff to develop collective expertise for deepening student learning.

The Path of Progress for Little Lake City School District

Little Lake City School District in Santa Fe Springs, California, is one of four K–8 districts feeding into the Whittier Union High School District. Over time, Little Lake City has established strong support systems for improving teaching and learning. Most school districts are unable to sustain a long-term focus and improvement strategies due to external pressures and the inability to develop a culture of continuous improvement. Little Lake City has proved to be an anomaly in that a "go slow to go fast" mindset has been embraced by district leaders, principals, and teachers to ensure that the continuous improvement of student learning results is the districtwide priority.

In the 2000–2001 school year, the state of the district was similar to many districts that had not yet transitioned to a standards-based instructional program. Each school, as well as every grade level, operated as its own entity. There was no consistency in practices stemming from the absence of standards-aligned curriculum and assessments, grade-level collaboration within schools, or vertical articulation between the elementary and the middle schools.

Focused attention on systemic improvement efforts began in 2001 when three schools entered state sanctions due to student academic underperformance. The initial work of these schools involved creating standards-based pacing guides with curriculum-embedded assessments and establishing collaboration time during the school day for teacher teams. In 2003, after two years of building foundational systems and practices in these three schools, Little Lake City began to scale the improvement process across all nine schools in the district. Over the subsequent five years, each school was able to establish effective professional learning community and Response to Intervention models, which led to a districtwide emphasis on high-quality teaching promoting commonly agreed-upon high-yield instructional practices within and among all schools. These systems, structures, and processes for districtwide support of teaching and learning enabled Little Lake City to more seamlessly transition to Common Core standards in 2011 and shift to local control and accountability in 2014.

The real test of a school district's ability to sustain improvement efforts occurs when leadership transitions, and in 2016, the superintendent who had led the long-term systems improvement retired. William Crean became the new superintendent after having served as a middle school principal and elementary school principal in Little Lake City during the past nine years of improvement. Maintaining the integrity of districtwide systems and determining how to sustain improvement efforts would be essential for ensuring continued progress for the school district.

The reality of Little Lake City was that the slow, consistent, long-term process of improvement had helped to develop and support a collaborative culture of continuous improvement. However, the systems, structures, and processes supporting teaching and learning were primarily led by district leaders and school principals. The next phase of systems improvement would have to be district-focused and site-driven: providing schools with defined autonomy that promoted a culture of leading from the middle and empowered teacher leaders to guide the improvement process.

In 2017, Little Lake City began its journey as a *District on the Move* by establishing School Academic Leadership Teams that would become equipped to lead coherent systems of continuous improvement at each site. Reflection on the Benchmarks of Capacity led to the realization that linking district goals to school priorities defined by the root cause analysis of student academic performance indicators would allow each school to define a strategic focus with clearly delineated improvement strategies for site-based professional learning. At first the process was disruptive in that schools were leading improvement efforts and beginning to recognize individually and collectively how best to improve on the district support systems for teaching and learning. This was a

(Continued)

(Continued)

shift from districtwide structures and processes that guided school improvement efforts to site-based decision-making for improving school practices and district support systems to achieve equitable improvement of student learning outcomes.

As Little Lake City entered year two of implementation in 2018, the focus among all school sites had converged on a common problem of practice: engaging all students in rigorous and complex tasks using high-yield instructional practices informed by timely assessments for learning. The School Academic Leadership Teams had begun to recognize that by clearly defining the focus of school improvement efforts based on the level of rigor and complexity (Depth of Knowledge Level 3; Hess, 2014) for student tasks, their collective efforts could focus on developing the collaborative expertise of teacher teams to co-lead robust collaborative inquiry processes for improving teaching and learning. Schools had established a more intentional focus on precision of pedagogy and instructional coherence driven by site-based student learning priorities. As a result, districtwide support systems were being adjusted and adapted in response to school site instructional priorities and the learning needs of students and grade-level teams.

The critical success factor for Little Lake City was focusing improvement efforts on school site priorities for equitable student growth that engaged teachers, principals, and district leaders in collaboratively developing precision of pedagogy to engage all students in rigorous and complex classroom tasks. This required refining multiple measures of student progress districtwide, refocusing weekly teacher team collaboration and monthly school-site data reflection sessions, and developing the expertise of school leadership teams, principals, and district leaders. The systemic improvement process at Little Lake City is evolving at the classroom, school, and district levels to create the strategic focus needed for improving teaching and learning that will ultimately translate into the equitable improvement of student learning outcomes.

Reflecting on Key Capacity-Building Strategies

- Collectively create a strategic focus for the equitable improvement of student learning outcomes by clarifying district goals and school priorities for student learning. This is achieved by focusing improvement efforts on the causal pathway that links student success indicators in classrooms to lead metrics for monitoring school academic progress that informs annual growth of districtwide academic proficiency.

- Clearly delineate improvement strategies that guide job-embedded professional learning by focusing efforts on a few student success indicators using high-yield instructional practices informed by timely assessments for learning. This defines the common work and support needed for teachers, principals, and district staff to collectively engage in the continuous improvement of practices and student learning results.

- School leadership teams design and refine an implementation plan that guides six- to nine-week school improvement cycles supported by district staff to develop collective expertise with deepening student learning.

Tips for Taking Action

Clarifying a strategic focus for the equitable improvement of student learning outcomes can become mired by two prevailing obstacles. First is overcoming what can be described as "analysis paralysis," which occurs when educators become overwhelmed, distracted, and confused by multiple sets of data, which leads to endless debate at the expense of informed decision-making (Birkinshaw & Ridderstrale, 2017). This results in superficial student learning challenges dominating the dialogue that prevents moving forward action steps to improve practices and student learning results.

Second is that writing an action plan is not the same as taking action. More often than not, a lengthy planning process for the creation of an action plan becomes the acceptable outcome of

(Continued)

(Continued)

well-intended improvement efforts. So the key to forward motion is co-authoring an action plan that clearly delineates strategies for leading short cycles of improvement occurring over the next six- to nine-week period of time.

A set of key questions framed as a School Implementation Plan (see Figure 2.2) has proved to be critical for school sites to move forward the improvement process through the leadership of the site principal, teachers, and district support staff. Such an action plan is collaboratively authored, communicated, implemented, monitored, and refined as part of recurring improvement cycles that guide the individual efforts of each school site and the collective efforts of the school district.

Figure 2.2 School Implementation Plan Template

Focus: Which schoolwide instructional priorities aligned with district goals will guide the improvement of student learning results?				
Outcomes: What measurable outcomes of student progress aligned with district goals will define the success of school improvement efforts?				
Student Success Indicators →	**Instructional Supports** →	**Schoolwide Support Systems** →	**Evidence of Learning** →	**Implementation Time Frame** →
Which student success indicators will result in the equitable improvement of student learning?	Which high-yield instructional practices and supports will have the greatest impact on student learning?	How can job-embedded professional learning be designed and refined to develop collective expertise?	How will evidence of learning inform the timely adjustment of classroom and schoolwide support systems for teaching and learning?	What time frames should guide our collaborative inquiry cycles to develop precision of pedagogy for deepening student learning?

© 2019 InnovateEd.

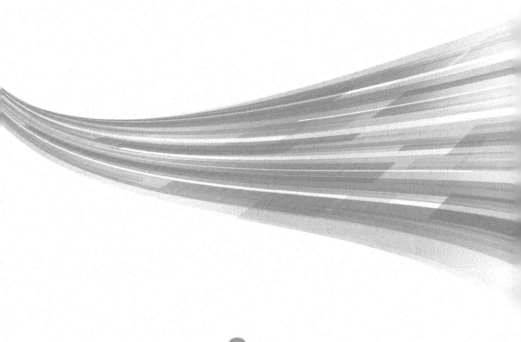

3

Culture of Shared Leadership and Systemic Collaboration

· ·

The book *Professional Learning Communities at Work* by Rick DuFour and Robert Eaker (1998) created a steadfast movement in education promoting collaborative school cultures focused on student learning with a results orientation. Rarely do you meet educators who have not heard of professional learning communities (PLCs) and, more often than not, have shared their journey of becoming a PLC. For many educators, school improvement is equated to the productive collaboration of high-performing teacher teams with shared leadership for improving the learning of all students.

For schools embarking on the PLC journey, there has been a tendency to focus on structural changes and team-driven processes as strategies for improving school culture. These play out as developing teacher teams, allocating job-embedded collaboration time, creating curricular units and common assessments, and analyzing evidence of student learning for tiered interventions. The role of a school leader can be transformed to management of these PLC structures and processes, which unfortunately occurs too often and can be counterproductive for creating a culture of continuous improvement. *Districts on the Move* expands on the shared leadership and systemic collaboration of the PLC movement by emphasizing the critical role of the lead learner.

Schools and *Districts on the Move* have formal structures and processes for collaboration, but have also cultivated leaders to serve as lead learners who shape culture by modeling co-learning and collaborating with staff to improve practices. This learning leader stance distinguishes managing structures and processes from leading cultural change and systemic collaboration. The direct benefit is fostering leadership from the middle that empowers those in closer proximity to student learning with leading the continuous improvement of school culture and practices.

Changes to structures and processes in the absence of lead learners cultivating leadership from the middle will not result in the sustainable improvement of student learning. Furthermore, to achieve long-term, districtwide student growth, the collective leadership of district staff, principals, and teachers serving as lead learners becomes paramount. This requires a shift from creating structures and processes for collaboration to developing leaders at every level that model co-learning and shape culture by navigating changes in practices for deepening student learning. The ongoing quandary is how best to develop systemic leadership capacity.

SERVING AS A LEAD LEARNER

Michael Fullan (2018) shared a compelling statement about leadership with district staff, principals, and teachers as part of a statewide school district collaborative in California: "Effective leaders see themselves as both experts and apprentices of the work at hand." In other words, leaders must possess knowledge that benefits the group and actively seek to learn from the group. This requires a combination of expertise and vulnerability.

The former is expected, but the latter is not openly accepted. Consider the last time you collaborated with a team or group, and reflect on how you led their efforts. Did you give advice or ask questions, provide solutions or inquire about options, coordinate actions or empower others to lead? Serving as a lead learner requires an inquisitive stance that promotes learning from within the group above leading the group.

This brings to light a consistent theme among leaders: the desire to have higher performing teams and more capable leaders within them. And yet there is not an equal measure of modeling by leaders to develop the desired skills and expertise within teams. "Practice what you preach" can be reframed as "model what you expect."

Lead learners interact with teams by modeling co-learning and shaping a culture that successfully navigates changes in practice to improve student learning. The desired outcome is developing the collective capacity and expertise within the group to co-lead the improvement efforts of the group. This is true whether the group consists of students, teachers, principals, or district staff. The most essential step is identifying the groups or teams whose collective leadership will most impact student learning outcomes.

CULTIVATING SYSTEMIC COLLABORATION AND CO-LEARNING

We've noted that teacher teams or PLCs are most commonly referenced as the key group for collaborative learning. Principals and teachers serving as lead learners can have a dramatic impact on improving student learning by developing the capacity of teacher teams to co-lead improvement efforts. However, additional layers of systemic collaboration and co-learning are needed for a school district to create a coherent system of continuous improvement. In addition to teacher teams, the most critical groups supporting collaborative learning are school leadership teams (SLTs), principal collaboratives, and a district leadership team (DLT).

School leadership teams engage principals and teacher leaders in co-leading professional learning that supports ongoing development of teacher team capacity within the school. Principal collaboratives provide opportunities for cadres of principals to cross-pollinate best practices and leverage their leadership to support growth within and among all schools. And the district leadership team functions as a guiding coalition of district staff, principals, and teacher leaders whose primary charge is adapting school site supports based on the learning needs of staff and students in their care.

When viewed as layers of shared leadership, it is the collaboration and co-learning among and between these groups that develop collective capacity and collaborative expertise across the school district. Three key questions should be considered to guide the process of developing systemic collaboration and co-learning.

1. Do current collaboration structures and team-driven processes support ongoing capacity building of the groups most critical for districtwide improvement of student learning?

2. To what extent does modeling of co-learning by lead learners shape the culture of these groups to successfully navigate changes in practice for improved student learning?

3. How does vertical and lateral collaboration and interaction promote learning across schools and between district leaders, principals, and teachers?

These questions are not simple and are designed to bring forward the complexities of developing a system of shared leadership. More importantly, these questions should not be contemplated in an insular fashion; rather, they are best used to capture feedback and insights from district staff, principals, and teachers to create a collective vision of both current state and future aspirations. This is essential as leadership is purely subjective when seen from vantage points ranging from the district office to the school site and the classroom. If the purpose of leadership is promoting a culture of leading from the middle, then every level of a school district has a distinct role in empowering and equipping those in closer proximity to student learning.

LEADING FROM THE MIDDLE

Hargreaves and Braun (2010) initially identified leadership from the middle as a high-impact strategy for large-scale education reform that focused efforts on the role of school districts in leading implementation across broad education regions. In California, this would be similar to a county office of education focusing efforts on developing the capacity of school districts to lead deep implementation of high-yield instructional practices for improved student learning results. As the work of *Districts on the Move* has evolved over time, the concept of leading from the middle has gravitated toward defining the leadership role with the greatest influence on both improving district support of school sites and adapting school site practices to improve student learning results: the school leadership team.

Most schools have a leadership team with a wide array of purposes and functions. These range from logistical meetings focused on school activities, information dissemination, and coordination of events to strategic sessions for planning site-based professional learning, analysis of schoolwide student learning progress, and reinforcement of key instructional priorities. The source of this variance is most often associated with the culture of leadership that has developed over time in the school district. Has leadership been defined as a role, a shared responsibility, or both? Does the relationship between district leadership and school leadership promote compliance and conformity or innovation with defined autonomy?

Leadership creates the culture of an organization, and in time, the prevailing culture will define the role of leadership. Jack Welch, former CEO of General Electric, offered this advice: "If you want to change the culture of an organization change the way it develops its leaders" (quoted in Zenger, 2017, para. 5). How, then, do school districts develop a culture of leading from the middle?

First, collectively define the purpose of leadership as serving as a lead learner to develop capacity and expertise within groups and teams. Then, engage in collaborative inquiry processes that promote shared leadership at every level for improving practices and student learning results. Last, cultivate leadership practices through recurring lateral and horizontal co-learning opportunities to develop a sense of collective expertise among teachers, principals, and district staff.

The transformation of a school district to a culture of leading from the middle is simply framed as shifting from a leadership hierarchy to a leadership huddle. There will always be a linear connection linking district leaders, principals, school leadership teams, and teacher teams to student learning in classrooms. The middle group is the school leadership team that is best positioned for principals to inform district support of school sites and for teacher leaders to facilitate teacher team collaboration focused on improved student learning. Developing a culture of leadership wherein lead learners at every level engage in systemic collaboration and co-learning to develop collective expertise for deepening student learning is a critical factor for school district success.

The Path of Progress for Hesperia Unified School District

Hesperia Unified School District serves approximately 21,500 students in the high desert region of San Bernardino County, California, with 15 elementary schools, three middle schools, three comprehensive high schools, and four alternative schools. The culture of collaborative learning in Hesperia Unified may be the strongest asset driving improvement efforts. Whereas many districts consider culture to be an afterthought, district leaders, principals, and teachers in Hesperia Unified recognize the true nature of the phrase *culture eats structure for breakfast*. Cultural change influenced by leaders at all levels of the district is the accelerator of improvement efforts, which has separated Hesperia Unified from other school districts, and it is why this case study was selected to garner critical insights.

The district experienced long-term success during the No Child Left Behind era in education, and although professional learning communities were embraced, many improvement strategies were pushed onto school sites due to the driving force of annual academic performance measures. Examples of which were pacing guides and benchmark assessments developed and implemented by teachers that were perceived as mandates that dominated collaboration time. Professional learning communities continued to be a key driver of school district improvement supporting the transition to new state standards, implementation of the 4 Cs (critical thinking, collaboration, communication, and creativity), integration of one-to-one instructional technology, and shifting to a project-based learning environment.

With the onset of new state accountability in California, Hesperia Unified recognized that capacity building was needed to improve district coherence and that the refocusing of district efforts should be driven by school teachers and principals. This resulted in the adoption of the 4 Cs as an instructional framework from which a unit of study template, teaching and learning rubrics, and single assessments were developed in collaboration with teachers and implemented at school sites. At the same time, the superintendent encouraged innovation, risk-taking, and new ideas. The Education Services division provided 4C walkthroughs to encourage dialogue among schools of site progress focused on 4C implementation. While this was a more balanced approach that promoted school autonomy, teachers and site administrators expressed a lack of direction in regard to improved student achievement.

At the beginning of the 2017–18 school year, Hesperia Unified began its journey as a *District on the Move*. District leaders asked schools whether they were confident in finding evidence that students were making the progress necessary to be successful. There was not a clear answer, and knowing the impact of the NCLB era on district culture, moving forward would require a more robust system of shared leadership and deeper levels of collaborative learning. The first step was to establish a district leadership team consisting of district leaders, principals, and teachers as well as principal collaboratives and school leadership teams. These new structures for more systemic collaboration dismantled the typical leadership hierarchies and created more open dialogue for improving systems, processes, and practices.

These collaborative structures guided the process of clarifying the district focus and developing schools' student learning priorities. Rather than district leadership defining effective practices and assessment measures, schools began to drive the refinement of pedagogical practices and determine assessments of learning that more clearly measured student progress toward learning outcomes. Acknowledging the need for improved literacy levels throughout the district, it was clear that the 4C work in the district, with focused attention on literacy development, could make a significant difference as more innovative practices were emerging across the district. The focus on developing deep literacy across the

(Continued)

(Continued)

curriculum through the 4 Cs and innovative practices became a catalyst for the collaborative work throughout the district and its schools.

The Coherence Framework and Benchmarks of Capacity became the primary professional development topics for site administrators during the 2017–18 school year. Leadership training focused on collaborative leadership, challenging mental models, cocreating strategic focus areas for schools, and navigating the change process within and among schools. As the year progressed, greater clarity was established districtwide by maintaining a consistent focus on student literacy through the 4 Cs and innovation. This focus began to permeate throughout DLT meetings, leadership meetings, principal collaboratives, SLT meetings, staff meetings, and PLCs, resulting in examination of pedagogy and accountability. Purposely, accountability was not overemphasized as an external driver; rather, accountability naturally became part of the discussion as schools began to collectively define internal measures of student progress.

A critical factor for greater district coherence was promoting the role of lead learners. This emphasis began at the district level with the superintendent and cabinet increasing the frequency of interaction and co-learning with school staff throughout the district. There was a commitment from district leaders to be active participants in the DLT process and share in the responsibility of mentoring and building capacity of school principals. These simple steps connected the leadership of district divisions to the moral purpose behind the mission of the district and the work within each school. The DLT process provided opportunities to engage in dialogue and co-learn with site administrators and teachers in direct relation to the vision of the district.

Principal meetings, referred to as Principals' Roundtable, and school leadership team meetings also needed to become more school site driven. The deputy superintendent of education services created the Principals' Leadership group comprising principals from different levels in the district. These principal-led meetings focused on school needs as expressed by the group and included presentations by lead principals to inform improvement of district support systems. As part of this collaborative inquiry process with principals, a new evaluation process was developed based on the Ontario Leadership Framework that further promoted district capacity building and coherence-making. This not only created alignment between the district's priorities and the principals' goals, but provided opportunities for district leadership to engage in regular dialogue connected to school site progress, which better informed district cabinet meetings.

The principal collaboratives also enhanced the impact of district systems by making clear connections to the ongoing improvement efforts of each school. School leadership teams became a key link for focusing districtwide leadership efforts on improving schools' student learning priorities. This resulted in further reflection on curricular resources, instructional practices, and assessments for learning. As practices came into question, a stronger inquiry stance was promoted rather than defensiveness or quick reactions to solve surface-level problems.

Meanwhile, the leadership structure of the extended cabinet began to address systems-level leadership by focusing on the role of district leaders in creating a collective vision as opposed to expecting schools to execute a vision from the district office. With the overarching theme of servant leadership, this cross-departmental practice provided a greater understanding of the contribution from the various departments and helped to build a stronger collaborative culture.

By year two as a *District on the Move*, district leaders and principals had developed a common vision and language for coherence-making. At the first principal collaborative of the 2018–19 school year, principals reported evidence that teachers were also actively engaging in creating coherence as expressed by the same vision and language. The transformation of district culture was beginning to show signs of permeating throughout the district.

Teacher teams have begun to question legacy pedagogy and assessment practices. Principals have listened to staff and encouraged

(Continued)

(Continued)

examination of practices and improvement of assessments measuring student progress. The dialogue among principals and district leaders has focused on investigating better ways to support schools. With a redefined focus on deepening learning and securing internal account-ability, Hesperia Unified is creating a district culture wherein state standards and annual performance assessments can serve as guide-posts for student learning growth rather than external judgments of schools, teachers, and the students in their care.

Reflecting on Key Capacity-Building Strategies

- Lead learners interact with teams by modeling co-learning and shaping a culture that successfully navigates changes in practice to improve student learning. The desired outcome is developing the collective capacity and expertise within the group to co-lead the group's improvement efforts. This requires an inquiry-focused leadership stance that empowers those in closer proximity to student learning to lead the ongoing improvement of school and classroom support systems.

- Systemic collaboration and co-learning are needed for a school district to create a coherent system of continuous improvement. This culture of shared leadership develops collective capacity and collaborative expertise across the district.

  - Teacher teams collaboratively design recurring three- to four-week learning cycles that engage all students with high-yield instructional practices informed by timely assessments for learning to continuously improve student academic achievement.

  - School leadership teams, comprising principals and teacher leaders, co-lead the professional learning that supports ongoing development of teacher team capacity in the school.

  - Principal collaboratives provide opportunities for cadres of principals across the district to cross-pollinate best practices and leverage their leadership to support growth within and among all schools.

○ A district leadership team, functioning as a guiding coalition of district staff, principals, and teacher leaders, collectively adapts and improves teaching and learning support systems based on the needs of school staff and students in their care.

• A culture of leading from the middle is created by shifting from a leadership hierarchy to a leadership huddle that empowers principals to inform district support of schools and teacher leaders to facilitate teacher team collaboration focused on improved student learning.

Tips for Taking Action

Creating a culture of shared leadership and systemic collaboration is dependent on how a school district integrates the structures, inquiry processes, and key practices of teams most essential for maintaining momentum to improve teaching and learning. The natural tendency is that each level of the school district gravitates to either controlling or delegating responsibility for the leading of improvement efforts. District leaders may formulate improvement strategies that are cast upon schools or, transversely, create high expectations with little guidance for how to improve practices. Principals can lead school staff in ways that range from prescribed conformity to directionless autonomy. And some teachers in a school embrace productive collaboration whereas others cherish professional isolationism. It is the absence of clearly defined team structures, processes, and practices that prevents school districts from developing the shared leadership and systemic collaboration essential for realizing equitable improvement of student learning outcomes.

The question is why this current state continues to pervade as the cultural norm in education. And the only rational answer is that school districts do not have clear strategies for cultivating a collaborative culture of co-learning. The first step, then, must be to clearly define the structures, processes, and practices of teams most critical for co-leading districtwide improvement efforts. The planning tool shown in Figures 3.1 and 3.2 is designed to provide guidance for initial action steps that set the stage for long-term efforts of systemic capacity building.

Figure 3.1 **Team Structures and Practices for Systemic Collaboration**

Levels of Leadership	ANALYZE Evidence to Focus Direction	DESIGN Strategies for Capacity Building	IMPLEMENT Action Steps to Build Capacity	REFINE Practices to Improve Impact
District Leadership	Set a few goals and outcomes to create a strategic focus for student learning	Create systems of support for leadership, teaching, and student learning	Develop collective expertise of principals and teacher leaders through job-embedded professional learning	Engage school leaders in problems of practice to collectively improve teaching and learning supports
Principal Leadership	Focus school improvement efforts on student learning priorities	Cultivate a collaborative culture focused on visible evidence of student learning	Provide time, resources, and supports to engage teachers in developing schoolwide instructional capacity	Review progress of improvement efforts with teacher leaders to improve schoolwide support systems
School Leadership Teams	Clarify root causes of student inequity and underperformance	Define student success indicators and evidence of learning to guide schoolwide instructional supports	Guide professional learning of teacher teams focused on the continuous improvement of student learning	Improve capacity of teacher teams to collaboratively plan instruction using evidence of student learning
Teacher Teams	Define gaps in student academic skills and behaviors	Create learning progressions that gradually release students to complete rigorous and complex tasks	Engage students in learning cycles with personalized instruction for mastery of skills and concepts	Monitor evidence of student learning to collaboratively improve student tasks and instructional supports

Figure 3.2 Action Planning Tool for Developing Systemic Collaboration

Levels of Leadership	ANALYZE Evidence to Focus Direction	DESIGN Strategies for Capacity Building	IMPLEMENT Action Steps to Build Capacity	REFINE Practices to Improve Impact
District Leadership				
Principal Leadership				
School Leadership Teams				
Teacher Teams				

4

Coherent Instructional Framework for Developing Collective Expertise

· ·

Developing collective expertise to deepen student learning is the foundation for equitable improvement of student learning outcomes. Richard Elmore defined this path of progress as the instructional core: maintaining high levels of student engagement in the learning of rigorous content supported by teachers with pedagogical expertise (City, Elmore, Fiarman, & Teitel, 2009). However, successfully engaging students in rigorous and complex tasks calls on teachers to integrate curricular resources with instructional strategies and assessments for learning in a way that supports the learning needs of all students.

Fostering such precision of pedagogy is best accomplished by creating a coherent instructional framework through job-embedded professional learning. This plays out as teachers, principals, and district staff engage in the collaborative inquiry of student learning progressions as part of recurring three- to four-week instructional cycles. Precision of pedagogy and instructional coherence are shaped over time through systemic collaboration and co-learning within and among schools.

The challenge faced by educators is that schools have been besieged by external measures of annual student academic proficiency rather than an internal focus and commitment to developing collective efficacy, a common belief in the collective ability to continuously improve teaching and learning. The impact has been that student success is most often defined by external measures of improvement rather than visible evidence of progress from the work produced by students in classrooms. If attention can remain on the student desk, then precision of pedagogy and instructional coherence will increase as educators collectively engage in short cycles of collaborative inquiry.

CREATING INSTRUCTIONAL COHERENCE

What is most critical for consideration is establishing the purpose of joint interaction among district staff, principals, and teachers in designing a coherent instructional framework. This can be perceived as either the task of creating a tool that informs instructional practices or an ongoing process of reflection for refining instructional practices, when in reality it is both. As can be imagined, the culture of leadership in the school district has a dramatic impact on the outcome of this joint interaction.

Here's the wrong approach for creating instructional coherence: provide all teachers with standards-based curriculum, training on instructional strategies, and access to standards-aligned assessments, then support schools with integrating instructional tools and resources to meet the learning needs of all students. As Fullan and Quinn (2016) have noted in *Coherence*, the outcome will only result in fragmented implementation and overload from lack of clarity and focus. Unfortunately, this is the approach taken more often than not in school districts: provide training and resources that inform teaching and learning. Creating instructional coherence occurs only through the collaborative work of educators focused on improving pedagogy. It is the specificity and precision of pedagogy that provide the clarity needed to create instructional coherence.

So where do you start? First, openly acknowledge that a coherent instructional framework will only serve as a guide for improving the instructional core: student engagement, content rigor, task complexity, and teacher expertise. Next, collectively recognize that precision of practice from the collaborative work of teachers, principals, and district staff will add depth and specificity to the instructional framework. Last, maintain a consistent focus on robust collaborative inquiry processes for improving the precision of pedagogy to meet the learning needs of all students.

Clearly, then, a coherent instructional framework is not about creating a product for dissemination. Rather, it is an ongoing process for improving the instructional core. This is realized when district staff collaborate with principals and teacher leaders to establish guiding principles that inform integration of curricular resources, instructional strategies, and assessments for learning to support the learning needs of students in every school. This process relies on teachers, principals, and district support staff engaging in the collaborative inquiry of three- to four-week instructional cycles to develop precision of pedagogy for improved student learning results. This ongoing interaction and co-learning ensures that a coherent instructional framework will continue to evolve in depth and specificity as precision of practice from within and among schools is shared and cultivated to strengthen the instructional core.

ROBUST COLLABORATIVE INQUIRY PROCESSES

In collaborative inquiry, educators work together by analyzing evidence of student learning to identify common challenges and test instructional approaches in an effort to develop collective expertise for improving student learning. This is not a once and done process. Instead, collaborative inquiry should occur throughout the school year in three- to four-week cycles that inform teaching and learning. Furthermore, collaborative inquiry is not only a process for developing teacher expertise, but it is mutually beneficial for district leaders and principals to improve systems of support for teaching and learning. Robust collaborative inquiry processes have the most impact on improving student learning when they are part and parcel of job-embedded professional learning among and between teachers, principals, and district staff.

Collaborative inquiry is the most critical aspect of achieving high-impact professional learning among educators. One approach is to engage in lesson study wherein teams of teachers collaboratively plan, teach, observe, revise, and share the results of a single lesson. A group of teachers researches and writes a lesson plan with expectations for how teaching students will result in better understanding of a certain concept. One teacher volunteers to teach the lesson while other teachers observe the impact on student learning. The group then meets to review the lesson and revise as needed for another teacher to be observed teaching the updated lesson in their classroom. The goal is to develop greater precision of pedagogy by observing visible evidence of student learning.

We advocate that this collaborative inquiry process can have equal impact by focusing on three- to four-week progressions of student learning. This can be accomplished by defining student success indicators, high-yield instructional practices, and timely assessments for learning that inform the pedagogy of teacher teams for an agreed-upon period of time. Engaging principals and district staff in this inquiry process allows collective insight to provide opportunities for ongoing reflection and feedback on student learning progress. The collaboration and co-learning among and between teachers, principals, and district staff makes for a robust collaborative inquiry process as it develops the collective expertise of the group. The power of collaborative inquiry is the focused effort of improving learning at the student desk, which in turn develops precision of pedagogy for deepening student learning.

DEVELOPING PRECISION OF PEDAGOGY

There is a well-known cartoon of a person stating they taught a dog how to whistle. The dog sits in silence, and an observer comments that the dog isn't whistling. In response, the person says, "I said I taught the dog to whistle. I didn't say the dog learned how to whistle" (Blake, 1974). And there's the dichotomy of teaching versus learning that is subjective from the vantage point of teacher and student. So what does pedagogy have to do with it? Pedagogy is the study of how knowledge and skills are exchanged during interactions that take place in the learning process—or simply put, studying the impact of teaching on student learning.

Developing precision of pedagogy is contingent upon the specificity of the learning intention. "Students will demonstrate the ability to read fluently (or solve multistep math problems)" is a vague learning intention. What is missing is the specificity of how knowledge and skills will be exchanged during the learning process through interactions between the teacher and students and among students. Collaborative inquiry plays a major role in creating specificity and precision of practice, which begins when a group of educators asks, "I wonder how we can develop our expertise to engage all students in successfully completing more rigorous and complex learning tasks."

Ultimately, this leads down the path of defining which aspects of the learning process are preventing more students from being successful. Note the emphasis on the learning process rather than teaching practices. One way to develop precision of pedagogy is by focusing efforts on what has been referred to as *target students*. In every school and in each classroom there are students who don't seem to make as much growth, progress in learning over time, and annual increases in academic proficiency. The intent is not to focus instruction only on target students. Instead, it is to identify a few students in each classroom that represent larger populations of students with similar learning needs and levels of academic growth. Then it's about clarifying the subtle nuances of student interaction in the learning process that will have the most impact on the students' ability to apply skills and concepts using content knowledge.

How do you know whether a school is progressing toward greater precision of pedagogy? It is defined by the culture of the school: the depth and specificity of dialogue among teachers and school leaders as they collectively develop expertise in support of student learning. This culture of learning in schools is best illustrated by the remarks of a school principal: "I knew we had established a culture of learning when I observed teachers exiting their classrooms between periods to share suggestions with their colleagues on how to adjust student learning in real time based on what had been experienced during the previous class period." Creating precision of pedagogy stems from the interactions and co-learning among teachers as they seek to understand the evidence of their impact on the student learning process.

The Path of Progress for Corona-Norco Unified School District

For the Corona-Norco Unified School District, being named a finalist for the Broad Prize in 2012 and 2013 served as a catalyst for engaging in the journey of coherence-making that would build on a strong system of schools to create a coherent school system. The district, comprising 50 schools with highly competent school leaders and well-equipped teachers, had been recognized for the long-term efforts of closing student equity gaps. And it is this relentless focus on accelerating the learning of all students that sets Corona-Norco Unified apart from other school districts. Without such an internal focus on equitable student growth, school districts will not be able to sustain efforts focused on developing instructional coherence and precision of pedagogy. This is a process-driven endeavor, and many insights into how to approach these capacity-building efforts are illustrated in this multiyear journey of continuous improvement.

The individual capacity of each school had allowed Corona-Norco Unified to serve students well. The next phase of district improvement would need to balance central office support systems with school improvement efforts so that a culture of defined school autonomy would further develop collective capacity to deepen student learning. In 2014, Corona-Norco became one of the first districts to join the network of *Districts on the Move*. Over the subsequent years, capacity-building efforts took the form of three distinct phases. During years one and two, an opt-in approach was offered for schools to participate in a site-based system of support. At this time, about 14 percent of schools were engaged in a structured support model combining principal coaching with school leadership team development to build capacity with leading six-week collaborative inquiry cycles focused on student success indicators, high-yield instructional practices, and evidence of learning.

This took the shape of a modified lesson study model wherein a school leadership team developed an implementation plan for leading cycles of inquiry to improve teaching and learning. The leadership team then participated in collaborative lesson design, engaged students in the learning process, and reflected on evidence of impact via learning rounds or student work analysis. This collaborative inquiry process was repeated three times throughout the school year, with opportunities for principals to receive coaching in support of serving as a learning leader of the improvement process.

By 2016, the Coherence Framework was beginning to be used by the district's Education Services to engage principals in assessing current district capacity and clarifying areas for improvement (Fullan & Quinn, 2016). The result was the creation of a District Systems Team comprising principals and district leaders with the common purpose of creating coherence of district systems through the lens of the four right drivers (focusing direction, cultivating collaborative cultures, deepening learning, and securing accountability). The opt-in model of support for schools continued, with 32 percent of school sites participating in site-based professional learning guided by school implementation plans for improving capacity to lead six-week cycles of collaborative inquiry focused on teaching and learning.

In their fourth year as a *District on the Move*, Corona-Norco established five principal collaboratives (grouping of principals into learning teams), which served as an effective structure for district leaders and principals to engage in robust collaborative learning around how to serve as lead learners of the coherence-making process both within schools and districtwide. At this point, 52 percent of schools had participated in the site-based system of support, which allowed participating principals to serve as leads for each principal collaborative as well as to inform the improvement efforts of the District Systems Team. Focusing direction through improved structures for systemic collaboration and co-learning provided the internal guidance needed for Corona-Norco to adopt a refined district vision of "literacy, math, and closing the gap through academic rigor and relevance and social emotional supports." This four-year progression of improvement also led to the collective understanding that a coherent instructional framework was a critical success factor for school sites to achieve equitable improvement of student learning through recurring six-week cycles of collaborative inquiry.

(Continued)

(Continued)

As of the 2018 school year, every school in Corona-Norco had established a site-based instructional focus based on the district priorities of literacy, math, and closing the achievement gap. In addition, 64 percent of schools had engaged in site-based support systems to build capacity of teacher teams with leading six-week inquiry cycles focused on student success indicators, high-yield instructional practices, and evidence of learning. However, district leaders, principals, and teachers had come to collectively recognize the need for a more coherent instructional framework to guide site-based collaborative inquiry cycles for achieving equitable improvement of student achievement in literacy and mathematics.

The collaborative work of the District Systems Team shifted to co-constructing a coherent instructional framework that would guide purposeful integration of curriculum, instruction, assessment, and learning climates for equitable growth of student literacy skills and mathematical practices. Guiding principles were created that linked a few key student learning competencies with critical academic skills and high-yield instructional practices. A process was established for engaging principal collaboratives with making meaning of the emerging instructional framework and providing feedback based on each school's current efforts to improve teaching and learning. Principals from all 50 schools were then able to support school leadership teams with adding depth and specificity to the instructional framework as part of site-based collaborative inquiry cycles focused on achieving equitable growth in student learning outcomes.

Corona-Norco's coherent instructional framework will continue to be adjusted and adapted based on the collective efforts of teachers, principals, and district leaders. In turn, the continuous improvement process, led by recurring cycles of collaborative inquiry, will further develop collective expertise with engaging students in rigorous and complex tasks using high-yield pedagogical practices and timely assessments for learning. Lisa Simon, associate superintendent of curriculum and instruction, provided the following reflection on this multiyear journey: "This work has been both professionally and personally important to me. I believe in it. I am invested in our collective journey of achieving greater coherence through collaboration."

Reflecting on Key Capacity-Building Strategies

- A coherent instructional framework informs school sites with integration of curricular resources, instructional strategies, assessment practices, and learning climates to guide district-wide improvement of the instructional core: student engagement, content rigor, task complexity, and teacher expertise. The collaborative work of teachers, principals, and district staff adds depth and specificity to the instructional framework as improved precision of practice is developed to meet the learning needs of all students.

- Robust collaborative inquiry processes guide job-embedded professional learning among and between teachers, principals, and district staff. This takes shape as three- to four-week cycles of inquiry for analyzing evidence of student learning, identifying common challenges, and testing instructional approaches in an effort to develop collective expertise with deepening student learning.

- Developing precision of pedagogy is contingent upon the specificity of how knowledge and skills will be exchanged during the learning process through interactions between the teacher and students and among students. Educators seek to understand evidence of impact on the student learning process by asking, "How can we develop our expertise with engaging all students to successfully complete more rigorous and complex learning tasks?"

Tips for Taking Action

Annual performance measurement of student learning is the primary driver of district and school improvement in the United States. Accountability systems at the federal, state, and local levels have further aligned as an integrated approach for monitoring the equitable improvement of student learning outcomes. And at the same time, there is broad recognition that annual growth in learning for all students is contingent upon the impact of high-yield pedagogical practices occurring on a daily basis within each classroom and among all schools. This points to a commonly agreed-upon notion

(Continued)

(Continued)

that reducing the variance in student learning growth is the true North Star that should guide systemic district improvement.

So how can school districts balance the pressure of annual student improvement measures with the short-term growth of student learning results in a way that promotes an internal focus on developing collective capacity and collaborative expertise? The key to such a long-term vision for success is to recognize that the improvement of practices always precedes growth in student learning results. Successfully leading the improvement of practices and student learning results requires a coherent instructional framework that guides robust collaborative inquiry processes for developing precision of pedagogy. The most effective method for school districts to accelerate internal capacity building is through the use of protocols that guide short cycles of instructional planning informed by timely evidence of student learning to continuously improve teaching and learning. What follows in Figures 4.1 and 4.2 are protocols that can be used to shape the beginning and end of a three- to four-week instructional cycle for developing precision of pedagogy to accelerate student learning.

Figure 4.1 Instructional Design Protocol

This is a process protocol for strategically designing lessons and tasks directly related to the standards and based on the schoolwide focus area.	
Opening 5 minutes	Review norms. Participants review the purpose and process of the protocol. Review focus: Connect to the School Implementation Plan.
Design the Learning Target 10 minutes	Design the learning target based on the following: • Selection of State Standards • Determination of DOK level *What is the explicit expectation for mastery of standards-based skills/concepts?* *What is the explicit expectation for level of cognitive application (DOK level)?*
Define the Performance Outcome 10 minutes	Define student performance outcomes based on the following: • Concepts and skills students must apply • Level of cognitive application • Student product/performance • Feedback to the student *How do your rubrics, exemplars, or models clarify expected student performance?* *Is there a clear connection between student performance and mastery of standards-based skills? Do the prompts/questions align with expected level of cognitive application?*
Develop a Sequence of Learning Tasks for Each Phase of the Instruction 30 minutes	Develop opportunities for student learning that do the following: • Connect to prior knowledge and build background knowledge • Promote development of literacy and critical thinking skills • Develop student metacognition • Support student collaboration and dialogue • Provide feedback to students as part of the learning process **Student Task, Guiding Questions, and Formative Feedback** *How does the task guide student mastery of skills/concepts and cognitive application? What questions engage students in deliberate practice of skills/concepts with scaffolding to support cognitive application?* *How do students actively engage in formative feedback to assess progress toward mastery of skills/concepts and level of cognitive application?* **Literacy Strategies and Engagement Strategies** *What are the student supports for close reading, evidence-based arguments, academic language, structured collaboration, and evidence-based writing?* **Targeted Student Support** *How are student group structures, questions, supports, and formative feedback differentiated based on levels of skill and concept mastery, cognitive application, active engagement, and social/emotional/behavioral needs?* *What specific support is provided to English learners, students with disabilities, and other targeted student groups?*
Agreements 5 minutes	Identify and discuss one to three specific strategies that each team member commits to implement.
Debrief 5 minutes	What did we gain as a team from the process? Discuss next steps based on School Implementation Plan. Set next date to discuss impact of the instructional design on student learning. Reflect on norms.

Figure 4.2 Common Assessment Protocol

This is a deductive tool to guide groups through analysis of data to identify strengths and problems of practice.	
Opening 5 minutes	Review norms. Review focus for the meeting: Connect to School Implementation Plan. If the common assessment was formative, also review the learning target. Reinforce the purpose and process of the protocol.
Defining Success and Challenge 10–15 minutes	Discuss and define criteria for success and criteria for student experiencing challenges.
Data Analysis Successes 10 minutes	Identify patterns from students that met the success criteria. • What patterns do we see? • Are there patterns by subgroups? Chart responses.
Data Analysis Challenges 10 minutes	Define challenge and identify patterns. • What patterns do we see? • Are there patterns by subgroups (e.g., English learners)? Chart responses.
Gap Analysis 5–10 minutes	Analyze the gap between successful and unsuccessful students. • What skills are successful students using? • What skills are unsuccessful students not using? Chart responses.
Synthesis 10–15 minutes	Synthesize the information from analyzing the gap between the skills successful students are using and the skills struggling students are not using. • What are the foundational and/or critical thinking skills all students need to demonstrate to be successful? • What skills are missing that might fill the gap? • Chart responses.
Learning Growth Target and Student Success Indicators 5–10 minutes	Revise Learning Growth Target based on analysis of student skills. If needed, include specific references to Student Success Indicators from the School Implementation Plan. • How will we know if students have achieved the Learning Growth Target?
Instructional Strategies 15 minutes	Connect to teaming Target and Student Success Indicators. • How have we already engaged students in the learning process? • How will we engage students to further support learning based on their needs? • What additional instructional strategies/supports could we use? Connect to research and instructional resources.
Agreements 5–10 minutes	Identify and discuss one to three specific strategies that each team member commits to implement. Set future date to discuss progress on agreed-upon student success indicators.

© 2019 InnovateEd.

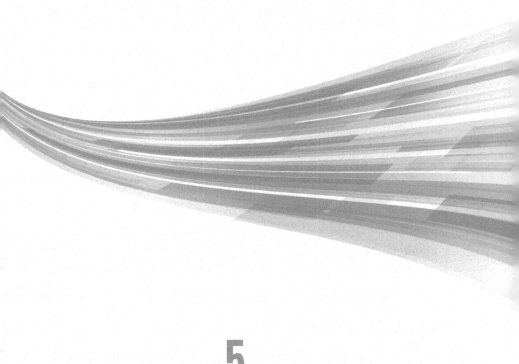

5

Evidence-Based Cycles of Inquiry for Continuous Improvement

· ·

We have found one of the most challenging endeavors for schools and districts is establishing evidence-based cycles of inquiry for the continuous improvement of leadership, teaching, and learning. The reason is the distinct separation of roles for teachers, principals, and district staff in leading improvement efforts. This relates back to the concept of leadership as a hierarchy rather than a huddle. District staff orchestrate resources and supports for each school to improve teaching and learning. Principals lead schoolwide improvement of supports for teaching and learning, and teachers work as teams within schools to improve instructional practices and student learning results. While all may be focused on improving teaching and learning, their collective leadership is not unified to create a coherent system of continuous improvement.

John Hattie (2015) has referred to this collective leadership as the process by which school districts develop collaborative expertise. Central to this concept is knowing which evidence best informs teachers, principals, and district staff of their collective impact on the equitable improvement of student learning outcomes. The research contends that the continuous improvement process strengthens when school districts establish annual student growth targets (lag outcomes), monitor progress with local assessments (lead metrics), and focus efforts on improving learning at the student desk (student success indicators). The essential question is: Which evidence informs the collective impact and continuous improvement among teachers, principals, and district staff: lag outcomes, lead metrics, or student success indicators?

We have found the evidence most often driving school district improvement is lag outcomes. This stems from a lack of coherence among the evidence connecting lag outcomes to lead metrics and student success indicators. There is a tendency to place higher value on either external annual measures of student performance or internal measures of ongoing student progress in classrooms. In *Built to Last*, Jim Collins and Jerry Porras (2004, p. 43) referred to this as succumbing to "tyranny of the OR" rather than embracing "genius of the AND." The improvement of a school system is dependent on creating coherence among the evidence that informs progress and impact at the district, school, and classroom levels: the collective impact of collaborative expertise.

So how does a school district develop a coherent system of continuous improvement through evidence-based cycles of collaborative inquiry? By establishing recurring feedback loops that promote frequent and timely sharing of evidence and impact of improvement efforts occurring at the classroom, school, and district levels. This begins with *knowing thy impact* from evidence of learning to guide the continuous improvement of practices (Hattie, 2012).

KNOW THY IMPACT

If the core groups in care of learning within a school district were assembled, then in a common room would be a cluster of students, teachers, principals, and district staff. Furthermore, if at the end of the school year each group was separately asked, "What do you believe has had the most impact on student learning?" then inevitably very different answers would be generated among these groups. Knowing thy impact begins with collectively establishing agreed-upon outcomes for the equitable growth in student learning. John Hattie (2015) has referred to this as every student attaining at least a year of academic growth for each year of school.

The notion of knowing thy impact, then, is grounded by a mutually understood outcome for student learning growth. A better question to ask is: "What is our agreed-upon impact on the equitable improvement of student learning outcomes?" And this should be asked at the beginning of the school year to create a common vision for the success of all students. Knowing thy impact is not an afterthought; it is a forethought. All too often the dialogue of impact is the last question to be asked rather than the first question of a collaborative inquiry cycle.

An example outside of education may shed light on having a commonly understood outcome in order to know thy impact. Southwest Airlines is the highest performing airline in the United States and has experienced forty-five years of profitable growth. But how? In 1972, when facing turbulent times and financial losses, Vice President of Ground Operations Bill Franklin was charged with solving the problems faced by Southwest Airlines. The solution was simply to unload and load passengers faster than the other airlines to get the planes back in the air: the now famous "ten-minute turn" (Hajek, 2015). The impact was that regardless of terminal location, airplane crew, or support staff, the collective outcome for knowing thy impact was whether the plane turned around in ten minutes. What is the lesson learned? Focus on the short-term indicators of student success in classrooms that predicate long-term annual growth in student academic achievement.

Evidence-based cycles of collaborative inquiry at every level of a school district always begin with defining the desired impact of collective efforts on the equitable improvement of student learning. And then proceed with a relentless pursuit to know thy impact on improving teaching and learning to discern which practices have realized gains in student achievement. Evidence of learning from within and among classrooms and schools serves as the key driver for continuous improvement of practices in a school district.

EVIDENCE OF LEARNING

It is important to broaden our thinking of evidence from monitoring student learning results to knowing whether capacity has improved to better support the learning of all students. The former is an indicator of student growth, whereas the latter is a benchmark of capacity. Research points to the fact that improved capacity always precedes growth in student learning. Thus, an essential question to consider is: What is the evidence of our collective impact on improving leadership, teaching, and student learning?

Imagine that a school district is focused on improving the lag outcome of annual student performance in literacy and monitoring student progress with the lead metric of quarterly English language arts benchmarks. Student success indicators have been identified by analyzing the root causes of variation in students' cognitive ability to apply content knowledge, specifically close and analytic reading and evidence-based arguments. Typically, these multiple measures of evidence would be used for monitoring student learning progress to predict annual growth in student literacy performance: monitoring progress to predict growth of a lag outcome. The problem is that the focus remains on the lag outcome as opposed to whether collaborative expertise has improved to support learning at the student desk. This is akin to chasing results rather than inquiring about collective impact from collaborative expertise.

Cycles of evidence-based inquiry should instead focus on determining which leadership and teaching practices will have the greatest impact on improved learning for all students. Or, put another way, solving the problems of practice that are preventing equitable growth in student learning outcomes. We are referring to problems of practice among students, teachers, principals, and district staff. Improvement of practice always precedes growth in student learning.

Five key questions can serve as a guide for engaging all levels of a school district in evidenced-based cycles of collaborative inquiry. These questions reframe the aforementioned district scenario of measuring annual lag outcomes, monitoring lead metrics, and improving student success indicators. The difference is how a collective focus for improving leadership and teaching is created through evidence-based inquiry about the desired impact on student learning.

1. What problems of practice are observed among students as they engage in the process of learning specific content-based skills and concepts? Which cognitive skills for applying content knowledge are most important for students' learning, and how will we know?

2. What problems of practice do teacher teams experience when engaging students in instruction designed to develop cognitive skills for applying specific content knowledge? Which instructional practices will better support learning, and how will we know?

3. What problems of practice do school leadership teams encounter when facilitating job-embedded professional learning of teacher teams? Which collaborative learning processes will better support developing the capacity of teacher teams, and how will we know?

4. What problems of practice do principals recognize as constraints for leading the improvement of school culture and practices? Which leadership actions will have the greatest impact on improving schoolwide supports for teaching and learning, and how will we know?

5. What problems of practice do district staff encounter when supporting principals and teachers in their collaborative work? Which improvements of structures and processes for collaborative learning will have the most impact on developing leadership capacity, and how will we know?

The common question "How will we know?" is meant to serve as an evidence-based feedback loop to inform the collective efforts of teachers, principals, and district staff in building capacity and improving student learning. Knowing thy impact from evidence of learning at the district, school, and classroom levels is foundational for creating a coherent system of continuous improvement.

CONTINUOUS IMPROVEMENT OF PRACTICES

John Kotter (2008), the foremost expert on leading change, has contended that a sense of urgency for change without clarity of focus creates frenzied activity with little productivity. Bryk, Gomez, Grunow, and Le Mahieu (2015), from their work in education with the Carnegie Foundation, have offered that more disciplined inquiry should drive improvement efforts. *Districts on the Move* have approached the disciplined inquiry process in a four-stage cycle: analyze, design, implement, and refine. Analyze root causes of the problem to create a strategic focus for improvement. Design high-impact strategies for building capacity to improve practices. Implement action steps with support, and adjust along the way. Refine improvement strategies based on the evidence of impact. Then, begin again the disciplined inquiry process of analyze, design, implement, and refine.

The challenge is the expectation of how fast practices should improve and how soon better results should be realized. Change is a process, not an outcome. Robert Marzano (2006), in the book *Classroom Assessment and Grading That Work,* has shown that formative assessment of student learning by teacher teams at three-week intervals is the threshold for achieving the highest gains in student learning. District improvement efforts are more impactful when implementation is reviewed at nine-week intervals because this provides time for schools to navigate the improvement of practices. This frequency also aligns with the traditional approach of administering benchmark assessments and generating quarterly student progress reports. To date, there has been little research on how frequently school leadership teams should review schoolwide progress to improve supports for teaching and learning. However, InnovateEd's action research in partnership with *Districts on the Move* has led us to advocate for a six-week timeframe.

This creates a compelling argument for integrating disciplined inquiry at the classroom, school, and district levels through three-, six-, and nine-week cycles of collaborative inquiry. At the conclusion of six weeks, after completing two three-week cycles of inquiry, the impact on student learning and improvement of practices among teacher teams would be shared with the school leadership team. This provides feedback for the school leadership team to understand the impact of schoolwide support systems, improvements in student learning, and focus areas for capacity building. Which, in turn, provides school principals with insights into emerging best practices based on evidence of impact and an opportunity to share progress and key learnings with other principals and district leaders as part of a nine-week inquiry cycle. Ultimately, these feedback loops give district leaders an opportunity to be immersed in evidence of learning from within and across schools in order to inform districtwide improvement of leadership, teaching, and learning supports.

Leadership is the unequivocal key for realizing this scenario of integrated inquiry cycles for systemic feedback. Not leadership as a hierarchy, but leadership as a huddle that stems from a culture of leading from the middle created by lead learners at every level. All of which goes back to a single question: How will we know our collective impact from evidence of learning to continuously improve our collaborative expertise?

The Path of Progress for Rosedale Union School District

Rosedale Union School District, located in Bakersfield, California, comprises seven elementary and two middle schools serving 5,800 students. Over the past nine years, the district has had stability in both district and school administration, which has guided a long-term focus on the continuous improvement of teaching and learning. For many districts, stability can lead to diminishing returns with a default toward maintaining the status quo. Rosedale Union, however, is an evidence-driven district that has demonstrated that improvement efforts can be sustained when there is a consistent focus that seeks evidence of the impact of practices on improving student learning.

In 2012, as California adopted new Common Core Standards, Rosedale Union recognized the opportunity to move toward a teacher-driven and student success–focused model of curriculum

(Continued)

(Continued)

delivery. As an initial step, district stakeholders, including school staff, administrators, and the Board of Trustees, developed a strategic plan to establish a common focus for refocusing districtwide improvement efforts. Over time, the district mission and philosophy came to be referred to as the Rosedale FOCUS (For Our Children's Ultimate Success), which had a commitment to three priorities: student academic growth, rigorous curriculum and high-quality instruction, and safe and healthy learning environments.

This strategic focus led to the adoption of three districtwide systems of support for teaching and learning: professional learning communities, direct instruction, and Response to Intervention. Soon after, a partnership with four local school districts was formed to develop units of study designed by classroom teachers that guided implementation of new state standards. And over multiple years, Rosedale Union strengthened systems of support for teaching and learning by developing common formative assessments, implementing research-based instructional practices, and engaging in collaborative instructional planning and data analysis.

Having developed districtwide systems of support, Rosedale Union began its journey as a *District on the Move* in 2016, and over a three-year period, it focused efforts on building school leadership capacity to sustain the improvement process. After collectively assessing district capacity and coherence based on the Benchmarks of Capacity, the district recognized clarity of focus and collaborative culture as core strengths. However, district systems, structures, and processes were driving continuous improvement, so establishing more robust cycles of evidence-based inquiry led by schools was needed to inform improvement of districtwide support systems. Such a focus on evidence of student learning would create more systemic feedback loops connecting student learning progress in classrooms with school improvement efforts and district support systems: a collective path of progress.

Improvement efforts centered around developing more systemic collaboration through cycles of inquiry among the district team, principal collaboratives, school leadership teams, and teacher teams. Every level in the district was focused on leading short cycles of improvement guided by school implementation plans that connected student success indicators with collaborative planning of high-yield instructional practices informed by evidence of student learning. Schools were organized into triads with district staff liaisons that served as cohort learning partners. School leadership teams and principal collaboratives were structured to engage in collaborative inquiry of student learning evidence for continuous improvement of practices and student learning results. In the words of Superintendent John Mendiburu, this further reinforced a culture of "we're all in this together" on a united and supported front to continuously improve student success.

Rosedale Union then adopted the slogan Know Your Impact to specifically acknowledge that each person in the district makes a difference for all students' learning and long-term growth. This was strategic in that team structures for collaborative inquiry needed to be driven by evidence of learning from student work produced in classrooms in order to more clearly inform the impact of instructional supports across all schools.

In year one, improvement efforts focused on developing the capacity of principals and teachers to serve as lead learners of school leadership teams that guided evidenced-based cycles of inquiry as part of job-embedded professional learning. As the capacity of school principals improved, the efforts in year two shifted to supporting teacher leaders in facilitating teacher team collaborative inquiry in three- to four-week instructional cycles and guiding the continuous improvement of school implementation plans based on staff and student learning needs. Having established more robust collaborative inquiry at the district, school, and classroom levels, the next phase for Rosedale Union was the integration of evidence-based inquiry cycles to create a more systemic improvement process.

(Continued)

(Continued)

The vision for the 2018 school year was to create feedback loops connecting evidence of learning from teacher teams and the improvement efforts of school leadership teams so that principals and district leaders could adapt and adjust support systems based on the needs of each school. The driving force for Rosedale Union is knowing the collective impact from evidence of learning to continuously improve collaborative expertise at the classroom, school, and district levels.

Reflecting on Key Capacity-Building Strategies

- Knowing thy impact is premised on a mutually understood outcome for student learning growth. A key question drives the collaborative work at all levels of a school district that should be asked at the beginning of the year to create a common vision for the success of all students: What is our agreed-upon impact on the equitable improvement of student learning outcomes?

- Cycles of evidence-based inquiry should focus on determining which leadership and teaching practices will have the most impact on solving the problems of practice that prevent equitable growth in student learning outcomes. The common question "How will we know?" is meant to serve as an evidence-based feedback loop to inform the collective efforts of teachers, principals, and district staff in building capacity and improving student learning.

- Continuous improvement is driven by the disciplined inquiry process of analyzing root causes of a problem to create a strategic focus for improvement, followed by designing high-impact strategies for building capacity, implementing action steps with support, and refining improvement strategies based on the evidence of impact on leadership and teaching practices and student learning results.

Tips for Taking Action

One of the most important questions in education is: What evidence will best inform us of our impact on the improvement of student learning? And the second most important question is: How will we engage in evidence-based cycles of inquiry to continuously improve our practices and student learning results? Unfortunately, these two questions have not become a cornerstone of the improvement process in education at the classroom, school, or district level. At the heart of this quandary is a lack of clarity about how evidence-based inquiry cycles can be integrated at every level of the district to guide improvement efforts. The simplest approach for solving this complex problem is through the use of lag outcomes, lead metrics, and student success indicators.

At the school district level, the lag outcomes of annual student performance serve as a benchmark from which to establish growth targets for improved student learning. Lead metrics at the school level, as defined by local assessments or evidence of learning, are used to monitor progress toward achieving the desired growth in student learning. And clearly defined student success indicators provide the guidance needed to adjust teaching that supports the learning of all students as part of three- to four-week cycles of instruction. Leading evidence-based cycles of inquiry at the district, school, and classroom levels require the integration of lag outcomes, lead metrics, and student success indicators for the continuous improvement of teaching and learning.

The following figures (Figures 5.1, 5.2, 5.3, and 5.4) can collectively engage district leaders, principals, and teachers in leading evidence-based inquiry cycles for the continuous improvement of practices and student learning results.

Figure 5.1   Measuring the Impact of Improvement Efforts

Source: scale: iStock.com/MaksimYremenko; rock and pebbles: iStock.com/Dmitry Volkov.

Lag Outcome: The measurement of annual student academic performance that serves as a benchmark from which to establish growth target(s) that define district/school goals and outcomes.

Lead Measure: The monitoring of progress toward achieving a defined growth target(s) that is measured by local assessments or evidence of impact on student learning.

Student Success Indicator: Clearly delineated academic skills and behaviors that are critical for individual students or student groups in attaining the desired growth in learning.

Figure 5.2   How to Monitor Evidence of Impact: Sample

Metrics that Matter	Frequency	Defined by Whom	Example
Lag Outcomes (annual growth)	Reviewed annually as a benchmark from which to set growth targets	District leaders, principals, and teachers via collaborative inquiry	Annual growth targets for literacy and math

| Lead Measures (evidence of impact) | Reviewed every nine weeks at district level and every six weeks at school level to monitor progress and evidence of impact | Districtwide lead measures defined by district staff and principals; school lead measures defined by principal and teachers | Quarterly benchmark assessments; end-of-unit assessments |
| Student Success Indicators (learning progress) | Reviewed every three to four weeks by teacher teams to inform the impact of teaching on student learning | Teachers with support from principals define the academic skills and behaviors most critical for student growth | Formative assessments that inform the impact of teaching on student learning results |

Figure 5.3 How to Monitor Evidence of Impact

Metrics that Matter	Key Actions for Districtwide and School-Level Evidence-Based Cycles of Inquiry	Goal 1:	Goal 2:
Lag Outcomes (annual growth)			
Lead Measures (evidence of impact)			
Student Success Indicators (learning progress)			

Figure 5.4 Time Frames for Monitoring Evidence of Impact

Month or Quarter	August	September	Timeline			
Lag Outcome	Annual math/ELA performance					
Lead Measure	Initial diagnostic assessment	Quarterly benchmark assessment				
Student Success Indicator	Student work analysis at three weeks	End-of-unit student task at six weeks				

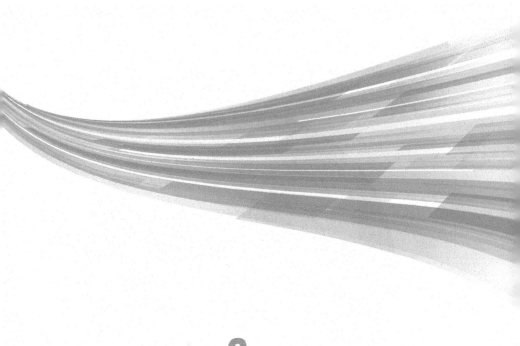

6

Leading a Coherent Path for Sustainable Growth in Learning

· ·

To create a meaningful context for leading districtwide systemic improvement, an appropriate analogy is the layered structure of an onion with scale leaves that protect and provide nutrients for the central bud from which roots germinate to support annual growth. Each layer of the onion emanates from the central bud, and then by design, life-sustaining resources flow back from the outer layers through the inner layers to the central bud. A parallel system exists in a school district wherein student learning supports are structured as nested levels connecting individual classrooms to

Figure 6.1 **Creating a Coherent Path for the Systemic Improvement of Leadership, Teaching, and Student Learning**

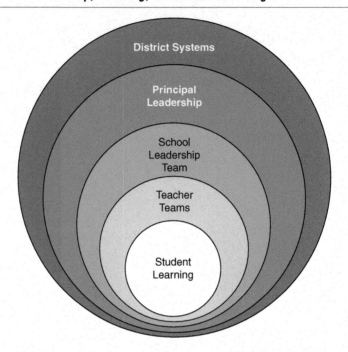

school sites and district systems. In a similar fashion, resources extend from the district level to the school level and classroom levels in support of equitable growth in learning outcomes for all students (see Figure 6.1).

A coherent path for the sustainable improvement of school district culture, capacity, and coherence requires a systemic approach that develops collective expertise at the district, school, and classroom levels. The Benchmarks of Capacity and integrated Leadership Competencies have illustrated the path of progress for creating a coherent system of continuous improvement. School districts can forge their own systemic improvement process by creating an action plan that guides the collaborative efforts of district leaders, principals, and teachers.

The Benchmarks of Capacity and critical success factors delineated in the subsequent rubrics can provide guidance for school districts to establish action steps for building capacity and creating coherence to realize the equitable improvement of student learning outcomes. We suggest using these rubrics to guide district leadership teams, principal collaboratives (cadres of principal teams or groups), school leadership teams, and teacher teams as they collectively engage in systemic improvement efforts. The power of evidence-based collaborative inquiry is realized through the collaborative dialogue and co-learning among and between teachers, principals, and district staff as they collectively strive to improve district culture, capacity, and coherence.

We advocate using a nine-week collaborative inquiry cycle to monitor internal capacity and systems coherence starting with establishing current reality and followed by recurring opportunities for reflection and refinement of the ongoing district improvement efforts.

RUBRICS AND PLANNING TOOLS

Critical Success Factor	Clarity of District Goals and School Priorities for Student Learning			
	Initiating	Developing	Accelerating	Sustaining
1. The analysis of multiple measures, including the performance of student groups, has guided schools to create a strategic focus for improving student equity, learning, and performance.	Schools have multiple plans, with multiple disparate goals listed, written to satisfy compliance with external performance expectations. Few, if any, schools have a clearly stated strategic focus that drives schoolwide actions. Fragmentation and/or competing priorities may cause overload.	Schools use annual measures of student performance to inform the selection of a strategic focus. Some, if not all, schools have a strategic focus that exists in formal documents but is not widely shared and does not drive decisions. Schools may have multiple plans, with goals listed, written to satisfy compliance with external performance expectations. School focus areas may not feel connected in a meaningful way due to some competing priorities.	Multiple measures of student academic performance and well-being are analyzed by schools to create a focus for improved student learning to achieve equitable performance outcomes. Most, if not all, schools have a strategic focus that exists in formal documents, is widely shared, and is beginning to drive decisions. School plans written to satisfy compliance with external expectations (SPSA, WASC, etc.) are integrated by schools to create a focus for improvement efforts. There is a strategy to reduce the number of competing priorities and eliminate distractors.	Multiple measures, including the academic performance and well-being of student groups, are analyzed by schools to create a focus for improved student learning to achieve equitable performance outcomes. All schools have a strategic focus that exists in formal documents, is widely shared, and drives decisions. It is clear how the strategic focus for schools is integrated into all plans (SPSA, WASC, etc.) to coordinate and leverage improvement efforts. A process is in place to remove distractors, base decisions on evidence, and build coherence year to year.

| | Clarity of District Goals and School Priorities for Student Learning | | | |
Critical Success Factor	Initiating	Developing	Accelerating	Sustaining
2. School implementation plans aligned with district vision and goals delineate coherent strategies that connect student success indicators with high-yield instructional strategies and assessments of learning that focus the collaborative work of teachers, principals, and district staff to continuously improve teaching and learning.	Principals and teachers have developed school implementation plans to comply with perceived district expectations. Improvement strategies may not be listed in the plan and are not coherently integrated. It is not clear how school focus areas are aligned to the district vision and goals.	Principals and teachers collaboratively develop school implementation plans to articulate their shared commitments. Improvement strategies connecting instructional practices and assessments of learning to student success indicators are stated in school plans, but are not coherently integrated to achieve the school focus and outcomes of improved student learning. Some school focus areas are aligned to the district vision and goals.	Principals and teachers collaboratively develop and revise school plans with strategies to improve student academic skills and behaviors. Improvement strategies consisting of high-yield instructional practices and assessments of learning are coherently integrated to guide schoolwide actions for improving student learning to achieve equitable performance outcomes. School improvement efforts are aligned with the district vision and goals and are driven by root causes of the gaps in student academic skills and behaviors.	Principals and teachers collaboratively develop and revise school plans based on an analysis of student learning at least every sixty to ninety days. The analysis of student learning priorities informs identification of high-yield instructional practices and refinement of assessments for learning, ensuring that improvement strategies are coherently integrated and guide schoolwide actions for improving student learning to achieve equitable performance outcomes. School improvement efforts are aligned with the district vision and goals and inform promising practices districtwide.

Clarity of District Goals and School Priorities for Student Learning

- Create a strategic focus for equitable student growth
- Clearly delineate improvement strategies
- Lead short cycles of improvement

Critical Success Factors	Action Steps
1. The analysis of multiple measures, including the performance of student groups, has guided schools to create a strategic focus for improving student equity, learning, and performance.	
2. School implementation plans aligned with district vision and goals delineate coherent strategies that connect student success indicators with high-yield instructional strategies and assessments for learning that focus the collaborative work of teachers, principals, and district staff to continuously improve teaching and learning.	

Culture of Shared Leadership and Systemic Collaboration				
Critical Success Factor	Initiating	Developing	Accelerating	Sustaining
3. Teacher teams, school leadership teams, principals, and district staff have collectively created formal structures and processes for systemic collaboration and co-learning focused on developing collective capacity to improve teaching and learning.	Formal structures or processes for districtwide and school collaboration and co-learning are limited or may not exist.	District staff, principals, and teachers have agreed on calendars for collaboration and are beginning to formalize structures and processes for districtwide and school collaboration.	Formal structures and processes for within-school and cross-school collaboration have begun to promote co-learning between schools and engage district staff in collaborative learning with schools.	District staff, principals, school leadership teams, and teacher teams have collectively created formal structures and processes for systemic collaboration and co-learning that guide six- to nine-week learning cycles that inform progress on the focus for student learning.

(Continued)

(Continued)

Critical Success Factor	Culture of Shared Leadership and Systemic Collaboration			
	Initiating	Developing	Accelerating	Sustaining
4. Teachers, principals, and district staff collectively support school improvement efforts by shaping culture, modeling co-learning, and using change knowledge to improve structures, processes, and practices based on the learning needs of all students.	Principals and district staff do not proactively or intentionally model learning themselves. Leaders do not apply knowledge of change theory to the improvement process. Collaborative work among and between district staff, principals, and teachers is fragmented, which promotes both a district and school culture of independent practice. Deep, trusting relationships are not present within and across schools, nor does a culture of trust exist between the district office and schools.	Principals and district staff support others that attend learning sessions, but rarely participate as learners themselves. Leaders rely on formal roles and structures to manage change. Collaborative work among and between district staff, principals, and teachers varies from shared responsibility to independent practice. Deep, trusting relationships are not consistent within and across schools or between schools and the district office.	District and school leaders participate as lead learners and are beginning to make learning for everyone a priority across the district. Leaders are beginning to see their role as developing others and creating structures and processes for interaction. Principals, teachers, and district staff are developing a culture of shared leadership focused on improving student learning. Collaboration and trust are emerging that promote sharing of promising practices within and among schools and with district leaders.	District and school leaders model learning by participating as lead learners of robust capacity building within schools and across the district. Principals, teachers, and district staff have established a culture of shared leadership focused on improving student learning. A culture of collaboration, deep trust, and risk-taking has been fostered at all levels to promote innovation and shifts in practice. Strong vertical and lateral collaboration and co-learning fosters sharing successful practices and embracing challenges as opportunities for deepening learning.

Culture of Shared Leadership and Systemic Collaboration

- Serve as a lead learner
- Cultivate systemic collaboration and co-learning
- Lead from the middle

Critical Success Factors	Action Steps
3. Teacher teams, school leadership teams, principals, and district staff have collectively created formal structures and processes for systemic collaboration and co-learning focused on developing collective capacity to improve teaching and learning.	
4. Teachers, principals, and district staff collectively support school improvement efforts by shaping culture, modeling co-learning, and using change knowledge to improve structures, processes, and practices based on the learning needs of all students.	

Coherent Instructional Framework for Developing Collective Expertise

Critical Success Factor	Initiating	Developing	Accelerating	Sustaining
5. A coherent districtwide instructional framework for job-embedded professional learning develops collective expertise with integrating curricular resources, instructional strategies, and local assessments to accelerate the learning of all students.	There is no instructional framework that connects curriculum, instructional strategies, and assessment across the district. Professional development is characterized by workshops and trainings offered in isolation and disconnected from school and district priorities. Schools comply with district improvement efforts without attention to staff or student learning needs, which creates a culture of fragmentation and overload.	The district office provides schools with curricular resources, training on instructional strategies, and standards-based assessments that are meant to serve as an instructional framework for student learning, though connections between and among them remain unclear. Professional development for principals and teachers consists of site-based workshops and trainings on practices that provide autonomy for professional learning but do not inform promising practices districtwide. Principals and teachers have autonomy in how instructional resources are utilized to engage students in progressions of learning tasks.	Teachers, principals, and district leaders have worked collaboratively to create a coherent instructional framework by integrating curricular resources, instructional strategies, and standards-based assessments. Teachers and principals at each school engage in job-embedded professional learning to develop collective expertise in high-yield pedagogical practices and assessments of learning. Principals and teachers are given district guidance and support with using instructional resources to engage students in progressions of learning tasks.	Teachers, principals, and district staff have collaboratively developed and periodically updated a coherent instructional framework that integrates curricular resources, instructional strategies, and standards-based assessments. Teachers, principals, and district staff collaboratively engage in job-embedded professional learning to develop collective expertise with engaging students in rigorous and complex tasks using high-yield pedagogical practices and assessments of learning. The focus of school improvement efforts provides defined autonomy for principals, teachers, and district staff to pursue innovative practices and develop collective capacity aimed at improving student learning.

	Coherent Instructional Framework for Developing Collective Expertise			
Critical Success Factor	Initiating	Developing	Accelerating	Sustaining
6. Robust collaborative inquiry processes ensure all students are engaged in rigorous and complex tasks using high-yield instructional practices informed by timely assessments of learning that results in precision of pedagogy and improved student achievement.	Collaborative inquiry does not reflect a full commitment to all four phases of the inquiry cycle (analyze, design, implement, refine). Individual teachers and some teacher teams have informal collaborative inquiry processes for instructional planning and reviewing evidence of learning. The rigor and complexity of tasks and precision of instructional strategies are not being refined to support the active engagement and learning of all students.	The depth and frequency of collaborative inquiry cycles vary among teacher teams due to lack of consistency in completing all four phases of the inquiry cycle. Collaborative inquiry cycles are becoming more focused on pedagogical practices and student engagement of more rigorous and complex tasks. Evidence of learning is beginning to guide teacher teams in improving instructional practices and clearly defining student learning outcomes for each inquiry cycle.	Teacher teams are becoming more intentional about each phase of collaborative inquiry, having structured processes for instructional planning, reviewing evidence of student learning, and developing more precision of pedagogical practices. School cultures of collaborative inquiry are developing as teacher teams engage in commonly agreed-upon inquiry processes. Some teacher teams engage in vertical articulation to inform teaching and learning.	Teacher teams within and across schools effectively lead collaborative inquiry cycles that guide ongoing, job-embedded professional learning. Structured processes for instructional planning and assessment for learning drive the continuous improvement of pedagogical practices and growth in student learning. Teacher teams, school leaders, and district staff collectively refine collaborative inquiry processes to support the continuous improvement of teaching and learning.

© 2019 InnovateEd.

Coherent Instructional Framework for Developing Collective Expertise

- Create instructional coherence
- Foster robust collaborative inquiry processes
- Develop precision of pedagogy

Critical Success Factors	Action Steps
5. A coherent districtwide instructional framework for job-embedded professional learning develops collective expertise with integrating curricular resources, instructional strategies, and local assessments to accelerate the learning of all students.	
6. Robust collaborative inquiry processes ensure all students are engaged in rigorous and complex tasks using high-yield instructional practices informed by timely assessments for learning that results in precision of pedagogy and improved student achievement.	

Critical Success Factor	Cycles of Evidence-Based Inquiry for Continuous Learning and Improvement			
	Initiating	Developing	Accelerating	Sustaining
7. Annual measures of student academic performance are used as benchmarks to establish growth targets monitored by local assessments that inform district and school progress with improving student learning outcomes.	External measures of student academic performance are reviewed annually to establish district and school goals for the school year.	External measures of student academic performance and well-being are used as benchmarks to establish district and school growth targets for the school year.	External measures of student academic performance and well-being are used as benchmarks to establish district and school growth targets that are monitored by local assessments throughout the school year.	External measures of student academic performance and well-being are used as benchmarks to establish growth targets measured by local assessments for frequent monitoring and communicating of district and school progress throughout the school year.

(Continued)

(Continued)

Critical Success Factor	Cycles of Evidence-Based Inquiry for Continuous Learning and Improvement			
	Initiating	Developing	Accelerating	Sustaining
8. Clearly defined cycles of collaborative inquiry, informed by evidence of student learning, create feedback loops at the classroom, school, and district levels for the continuous improvement of practices and student learning results.	Analysis of evidence of student learning is dependent on district scheduled events and/or is dependent on district assessments. Cycles of inquiry may occur at either the school or district level but do not inform the continuous improvement of practices across the district.	District and school scheduled events for analyzing evidence of student learning guide teacher teams, principals, and district staff in reviewing student performance on district and school assessments. Cycles of collaborative inquiry occur at schools and at the district office but do not inform one another. No feedback loop exists. There is limited sharing of progress and improvement of practices across schools and between schools and the district.	Cycles of collaborative inquiry among and between teacher teams, school leadership teams, principals, and district staff are informed by district and school lead metrics that guide the next cycle of inquiry with a common focus on accelerating student learning. There are structured opportunities for sharing progress and improving practices across schools and between schools and the district. Feedback loops, generated by inquiry cycles, are beginning to demonstrate some evidence of improvement of staff practices and impact on student learning results.	Cycles of collaborative inquiry among and between teacher teams, school leadership teams, principals, and district staff create feedback loops of the impact of improvement efforts on student learning results that guides the refinement of district services, school supports, and classroom practices for the next cycle of inquiry with a common focus on accelerating growth in learning for all students. Evidence demonstrates measurable improvement of staff practices and improved student learning outcomes.

Cycles of Evidence-Based Inquiry for Continuous Learning and Improvement

- Know thy impact on equitable student learning outcomes
- Focus evidence of learning on problems of practice
- Continuously improve practices through disciplined inquiry

Critical Success Factors	Action Steps
7. Annual measures of student academic performance and well-being are used as benchmarks to establish growth targets monitored by local assessments that inform district and school progress with improving student learning outcomes.	
8. Clearly defined cycles of collaborative inquiry, informed by evidence of student learning, create feedback loops at the classroom, school, and district levels for the continuous improvement of practices and student learning results.	

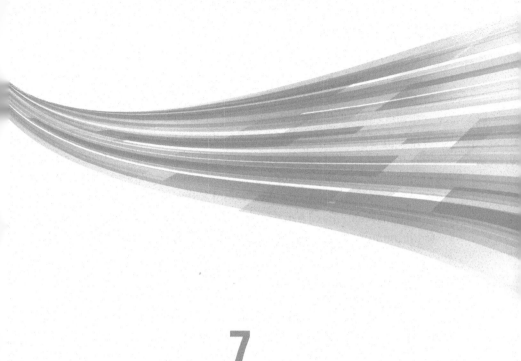

7

Building Capacity to Lead Systemic Improvement

·····························

W hy do so few school districts experience sustainable growth of internal capacity and student learning results, and over time become beacons of light for other districts to conceive equal levels of success? We believe the answer is found in the approach taken by school districts for leading the long-term improvement of district culture, capacity, and coherence. Beginning in 2014, the moral imperative and common vision of *Districts on the Move* was building capacity at the classroom, school, and district levels to achieve equitable growth of student learning outcomes. The ultimate question driving this collaborative work was: How do school districts create a coherent system of continuous improvement?

Over a five-year period of robust school district capacity building, the critical roles of district staff, principals, and teachers were codified to create the Benchmarks of Capacity, Leadership Competencies, and rubrics for reflecting on systemic improvement. The integration of district systems, principal leadership, school leadership teams, and teacher teams was clearly defined to shape the critical success factors for creating a coherent systemic of continuous improvement. The emergent theme separating sustainable improvement of a few school districts from recurring cycles of short-term solutions of a majority of school districts is the intentionally systemic improvement of culture, capacity, and coherence. This critical synergistic relationship between district culture, capacity, and coherence calls on leaders at all levels to collectively guide the long-term process of systemic improvement.

Leading systemic district improvement is best achieved through robust collaborative inquiry processes at the classroom, school, and district levels that support the continuous improvement of practices and student learning results. In the same manner that the layered structure of an onion protects and provides nutrients for the core bud from which life germinates, the nested levels of leadership within a school district provide the teaching and learning supports needed to realize the equitable improvement of student learning outcomes. Each of these levels of support within a school district plays a critical role in the systemic improvement of culture, capacity, and coherence-making.

District leaders establish a few goals and outcomes that guide school improvement efforts with a strategic focus for improved student learning priorities. Systems of support for leadership, teaching, and student learning are created to develop the collective expertise of principals and teachers as part of job-embedded professional learning. District leaders engage schools in overcoming problems of practice to collectively improve systems of support for teaching and learning.

Principals focus school improvement efforts on student learning priorities by cultivating a collaborative culture driven by visible evidence of student learning. Teachers are engaged in the process of allocating time, resources, and supports for developing schoolwide instructional capacity. The progress of improvement efforts is reviewed with teachers to adjust schoolwide support systems based on student learning needs.

School leadership teams clarify the root causes of student inequity and underperformance to clearly delineate improvement strategies that connect student success indicators with evidence of learning. This process creates specificity and precision of the schoolwide focus that guides job-embedded professional learning among teacher teams for developing collective expertise with collaborative instructional planning driven by evidence of student learning.

Teacher teams define the gaps in student academic skills and behaviors to create learning progressions that gradually release students to successfully complete rigorous and complex tasks. Students are engaged in learning cycles with personalized instruction that supports mastery of academic skills and concepts. Additionally, monitoring evidence of student learning guides teacher teams in developing precision of pedagogy for the continuous improvement of student learning results.

As school districts aspire to achieve equitable growth of student learning outcomes through the long-term improvement of culture, capacity, and coherence, the path of progress forged by *Districts on the Move* can serve as a road map for creating a coherent system of continuous improvement. The journey of each school district will be unique due to the complexities of whole-systems change; however, by leading a systemic improvement process, every school district can create a coherent path with a convergent focus on capacity building and coherence-making for sustainable improvement of student learning.

References

Birkinshaw, J., & Ridderstrale, J. (2017). *Fast/forward: Make your company fit for the future.* Redwood City, CA: Stanford University Press.

Blake, B. (1974). Tiger Daily Comic Strip, King Features Syndicate.

Bryk, A., Gomez, L., Grunow, A., & Le Mahieu, P. (2015). *Learning to improve: How America's schools can get better at getting better.* Cambridge, MA: Harvard Education Press.

City, E., Elmore, R., Fiarman, S., & Teitel, L. (2009). *Instructional rounds in education: A network approach to improving teaching and learning.* Cambridge, MA: Harvard Education Press.

Collins, J., & Porras, J. (2004). *Built to last: Successful habits of visionary companies.* New York, NY: HarperCollins.

DuFour, R., & Eaker, R. (1998). *Professional learning communities at work: Best practices for enhancing student achievement.* Bloomington, IN: Solution Tree.

Fullan, M. (2011). *Choosing the wrong drivers for whole system reform* (Seminar Series Paper No. 204). East Melbourne, Victoria, Australia: Centre for Strategic Education.

Fullan, M. (2018). *Leading coherence.* Presentation at the Second Annual Districts on the Move Summit, Smartsville, CA.

Fullan, M., & Quinn, J. (2016). *Coherence: The right drivers in action for schools, districts, and systems.* Thousand Oaks, CA: Corwin.

Hajek, D. (2015, June 28). The man who saved southwest airlines with a "10-minute" idea. National Public Radio. Retrieved from http://www.npr.org

Hargreaves, A., & Braun, H. (2010). *Leading for all.* Oakville, Ontario, Canada: Council of Ontario Directors of Education.

Hattie, J. (2012). *Visible learning for teachers: Maximizing impact for learning.* New York, NY: Routledge.

Hattie, J. (2015). *What works best in education: The politics of collaborative expertise*. London, England: Pearson.

Hess, K. (2014). Cognitive rigor and depth of knowledge. Retrieved from https://www.karin-hess.com/cognitive-rigor-and-dok

Kotter, J. (2008). *A sense of urgency*. Boston, MA: Harvard Business School.

Marzano, R. (2006). *Classroom assessment and grading that work*. Alexandria, VA: Association for Supervision and Curriculum Development.

Pfeffer, J., & Sutton, R. (2000). *The knowing-doing gap: How smart companies turn knowledge into action*. Boston, MA: President and Fellows Harvard College.

Westover, J. (2018). *Districts on the move: Getting serious about capacity building*. Smartsville, CA: InnovateEd.

Zenger, J. (2017, November 25). Change your leaders to change your culture. *Forbes*. Retrieved from http://www.forbes.com/

Index

Leadership That Makes an Impact

LYN SHARRATT
Explore 14 essential parameters to guide system and school leaders toward building powerful collaborative learning cultures.

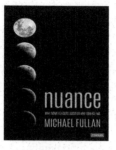

MICHAEL FULLAN
How do you break the cycle of surface-level change to tackle complex challenges? *Nuance* is the answer.

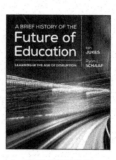

IAN JUKES & RYAN L. SCHAAF
The digital environment has radically changed how students need to learn. Get ready to be challenged to accommodate today's learners.

ERIC SHENINGER
Lead for efficacy in these disruptive times! Cultivating school culture focused on the achievement of students while anticipating change is imperative.

JOANNE MCEACHEN & MATTHEW KANE
Getting at the heart of what matters for students is key to deeper learning that connects with their lives.

LEE G. BOLMAN & TERRENCE E. DEAL
Sometimes all it takes to solve a problem is to reframe it by listening to wise advice from a trusted mentor.

PETER M. DEWITT
This go-to guide is written for coaches, leaders looking to be coached, and leaders interested in coaching burgeoning leaders.

ANTHONY KIM & ALEXIS GONZALES-BLACK
Designed to foster flexibility and continuous innovation, this resource expands cutting-edge management and organizational techniques to empower schools with the agility and responsiveness vital to their new environment.

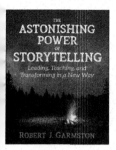

A SAGE Publishing Company

CORWIN HAS ONE MISSION: to enhance education through intentional professional learning.

We build long-term relationships with our authors, educators, clients, and associations who partner with us to develop and continuously improve the best evidence-based practices that establish and support lifelong learning.

InnovateEd

Building Capacity.

The mission of InnovateEd is developing school district capacity for the sustainable improvement of leadership, teaching and student learning.